First Workshop on Aggregating and Analysing Crowdsourced Annotations for NLP (AnnoNLP 2019)

Hong Kong, China
3 November 2019

ISBN: 978-1-7138-0075-0

Printed from e-media with permission by:

Curran Associates, Inc.
57 Morehouse Lane
Red Hook, NY 12571

Association for Computational Linguistics
209 N. Eighth Street
Stroudsburg, Pennsylvania 18360

Phone: 1-570-476-8006
Fax: 1-570-476-0860

acl@aclweb.org

Additional copies of this publication are available from:

Curran Associates, Inc.
57 Morehouse Lane
Red Hook, NY 12571 USA
Phone: 845-758-0400
Fax: 845-758-2633
Email: curran@proceedings.com
Web: www.proceedings.com

EMNLP 2019

Aggregating and Analysing Crowdsourced Annotations for NLP

Proceedings of the First Workshop on Aggregating and Analysing Crowdsourced Annotations for NLP (AnnoNLP)

November 3rd, 2019
Hong Kong, China

Introduction

Welcome to the First Workshop on Aggregating and Analysing Crowdsourced Annotations for NLP. We received 16 submissions and we accepted 7 of them. We are excited to also include two invited talks and one spotlight presentation.

Crowdsourcing, whether through microwork platforms or through Games with a Purpose, is increasingly used as an alternative to traditional expert annotation, achieving comparable annotation quality at lower cost and offering greater scalability. The NLP community has enthusiastically adopted crowdsourcing to support work in tasks such as coreference resolution, sentiment analysis, textual entailment, named entity recognition, word similarity, word sense disambiguation, and many others. This interest has also resulted in the organization of a number of workshops at ACL and elsewhere, from as early as "The People's Web meets NLP" in 2009. These days, general purpose research on crowdsourcing can be presented at HCOMP or CrowdML, but the need for workshops more focused on the use of crowdsourcing in NLP remains. In particular, NLP-specific methods are typically required for the task of aggregating the interpretations provided by the annotators.

Most existing work on aggregation methods is based on a common set of assumptions: 1) independence between the true classes, 2) the set of classes the coders can choose from is fixed across the annotated items, and 3) there is one true class per item. However, for many NLP tasks such assumptions are not entirely appropriate. For example, sequence labelling tasks (e.g., NER, tagging) have an implicit inter-label dependence. In other tasks such as coreference the labels the coders can choose from are not fixed but depend on the mentions from each document. Furthermore, in many NLP tasks, the data items can have more than one interpretation. Such cases of ambiguity also affect the reliability of existing gold standard datasets (often labelled with a single interpretation even though expert disagreement is a well-known issue). This former point motivates the research on alternative, complementary evaluation methods, but also the development of multi-label datasets.

The workshop aims to bring together researchers interested in methods for aggregating and analysing crowdsourced data for NLP-specific tasks which relax the aforementioned assumptions. We also invited work on ambiguous, subjective or complex annotation tasks which received less attention in the literature.

We would like to thank the program committee, all authors and invited speakers, and hope you enjoy the workshop.

Silviu Paun and Dirk Hovy
November 2019

Organizers:

Silviu Paun, Queen Mary University of London
Dirk Hovy, Bocconi University

Program Committee:

Beata Beigman Klebanov, Princeton (USA)
Bob Carpenter, Columbia University (USA)
Jon Chamberlain, University of Essex (UK)
Anca Dumitrache, Vrije Universiteit Amsterdam (Netherlands)
Paul Felt, IBM (USA)
Udo Kruschwitz, University of Essex (UK)
Matthew Lease, University of Texas at Austin (USA)
Massimo Poesio, Queen Mary University of London (UK)
Edwin Simpson, Technische Universität Darmstadt (Germany)
Henning Wachsmuth, Universität Paderborn (Germany)

Additional Reviewers:

Chris Madge, Queen Mary University of London (UK)
Juntao Yu, Queen Mary University of London (UK)

Invited Speaker:

Jordan Boyd-Graber, University of Maryland (USA)
Edwin Simpson, Technische Universität Darmstadt (Germany)

Table of Contents

Dependency Tree Annotation with Mechanical Turk
Stephen Tratz 1

Word Familiarity Rate Estimation Using a Bayesian Linear Mixed Model
Masayuki Asahara 6

Leveraging syntactic parsing to improve event annotation matching
Camiel Colruyt, Orphée De Clercq and Véronique Hoste 15

A Dataset of Crowdsourced Word Sequences: Collections and Answer Aggregation for Ground Truth Creation
Jiyi Li and Fumiyo Fukumoto 24

Crowd-sourcing annotation of complex NLU tasks: A case study of argumentative content annotation
Tamar Lavee, Lili Kotlerman, Matan Orbach, Yonatan Bilu, Michal Jacovi, Ranit Aharonov and Noam Slonim 29

Computer Assisted Annotation of Tension Development in TED Talks through Crowdsourcing
Seungwon Yoon, Wonsuk Yang and Jong Park 39

CoSSAT: Code-Switched Speech Annotation Tool
Sanket Shah, Pratik Joshi, Sebastin Santy and Sunayana Sitaram 48

Conference Program

Sunday, November 3, 2019

9:00–10:30 Session 1

09:00–09:10 *Welcome remarks*

09:10–10:10 *Invited Talk*
Jordan Boyd-Graber, University of Maryland

10:10–10:30 *Dependency Tree Annotation with Mechanical Turk*
Stephen Tratz

10:30–11:00 Coffee Break

11:00–12:20 Session 2

11:00–11:30 *Word Familiarity Rate Estimation Using a Bayesian Linear Mixed Model*
Masayuki Asahara

11:30–12:00 *Leveraging syntactic parsing to improve event annotation matching*
Camiel Colruyt, Orphée De Clercq and Véronique Hoste

12:00–12:20 *A Dataset of Crowdsourced Word Sequences: Collections and Answer Aggregation for Ground Truth Creation*
Jiyi Li and Fumiyo Fukumoto

Sunday, November 3, 2019 (continued)

12:20–14:00 Lunch break

14:00–15:20 Session 3

14:00–15:00 *Invited Talk*
Edwin Simpson, Technische Universität Darmstadt

15:00–15:20 *Distance-based Consensus Modeling for Complex Annotations*
Alexander Braylan and Matthew Lease

15:20–16:00 Afternoon coffee break

16:00–17:20 Session 4

16:00–16:30 *Crowd-sourcing annotation of complex NLU tasks: A case study of argumentative content annotation*
Tamar Lavee, Lili Kotlerman, Matan Orbach, Yonatan Bilu, Michal Jacovi, Ranit Aharonov and Noam Slonim

16:30–17:00 *Computer Assisted Annotation of Tension Development in TED Talks through Crowdsourcing*
Seungwon Yoon, Wonsuk Yang and Jong Park

17:00–17:20 *CoSSAT: Code-Switched Speech Annotation Tool*
Sanket Shah, Pratik Joshi, Sebastin Santy and Sunayana Sitaram

Dependency Tree Annotation with Mechanical Turk

Stephen Tratz
CCDC Army Research Laboratory
Adelphi, Maryland 20783 USA
stephen.c.tratz.civ@mail.mil

Abstract

Crowdsourcing is frequently employed to quickly and inexpensively obtain valuable linguistic annotations but is rarely used for parsing, likely due to the perceived difficulty of the task and the limited training of the available workers. This paper presents what is, to the best of our knowledge, the first published use of Mechanical Turk (or similar platform) to crowdsource parse trees. We pay Turkers to construct unlabeled dependency trees for 500 English sentences using an interactive graphical dependency tree editor, collecting 10 annotations per sentence. Despite not requiring any training, several of the more prolific workers meet or exceed 90% attachment agreement with the Penn Treebank (PTB) portion of our data, and, furthermore, for 72% of these PTB sentences, at least one Turker produces a perfect parse. Thus, we find that, supported with a simple graphical interface, people with presumably no prior experience can achieve surprisingly high degrees of accuracy on this task. To facilitate research into aggregation techniques for complex crowdsourced annotations, we publicly release our annotated corpus.

1 Introduction

State of the art parsing models, which are important components to countless natural language processing workflows, are trained using treebanks of manually annotated parse trees. Unfortunately, many languages do not have treebanks and even the treebanks that do exist possess significant limitations in terms of size, genre, style, topic coverage, and/or other dimensions. Even the venerable Penn Treebank (Marcus et al., 1993)—one of the largest and most widely used treebanks—contains examples from only a single news source. Expanding existing treebanks or creating new ones tends to be quite expensive; for instance, the Prague Dependency Treebank, with over a million syntactically linked words, cost approximately $600,000 (Böhmová et al., 2003). In this work, we explore the use of crowdsourcing both to mitigate this cost barrier and also because, perhaps more importantly, it serves as a proof-of-concept for the case in which only non-experts are available to produce the parse trees, which is likely to be the situation for most under-resourced languages. Despite the widespread use of crowdsourcing to collect linguistic annotations, there have been few efforts to apply crowdsourcing to parsing—a fact we believe is largely due to concerns about the complexity of the task, the training requirements for the workers, as well as the skillfulness, diligence, and consistency of workers on crowdsourcing platforms such as Mechanical Turk.

This paper presents what is, to the best of our knowledge, the first use of Mechanical Turk or similar platform to crowdsource dependency parse trees. We request 10 annotations for each of 500 trees (250 from the Penn Treebank (PTB) and 250 from Wikipedia) and find that, despite not requiring any form of training, several of the Turkers who annotate 50 or more PTB sentences achieve at least 90% attachment agreement with the dependency conversion reference trees. Furthermore, for 72% of the PTB sentences, at least one Turker produces a tree that fully matches the reference. Ultimately, these results establish a baseline for what people with presumably no prior training can achieve in performing this challenging task.

2 Approach

To collect dependency tree annotations, we use Mechanical Turk's *external question* HIT (Human Intelligence Task) functionality. HITs are the basic unit of work on Mechanical Turk; essentially, they are questions to be answered, with an associated monetary reward. In the case of *external question*

Proceedings of the First Workshop on Aggregating and Analysing Crowdsourced Annotations for NLP, pages 1–5
Hong Kong, China, November 3, 2019. ©2019 Association for Computational Linguistics
https://doi.org/10.18653/v1/P17

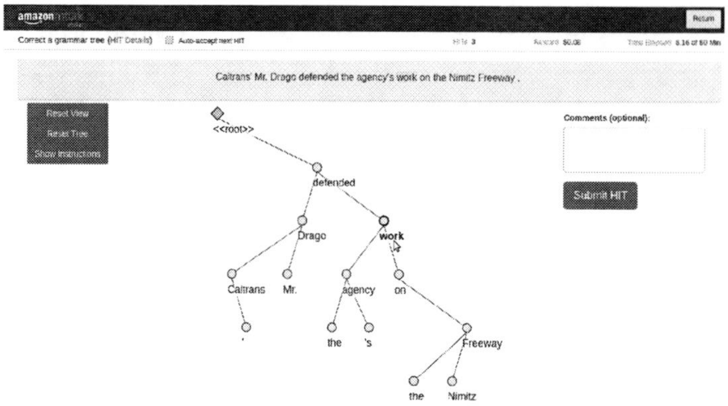

Figure 1: Screenshot of our annotation interface in the Mechanical Turk sandbox.

HITs, the annotation interface is hosted on an external website, which is embedded on the Mechanical Turk page within an HTML *iframe*. Each of our HITs involves constructing an unlabeled[1] dependency tree for a single sentence using the annotation interface described below. When Turkers submit their work, it goes both to the external server and to Amazon's Mechanical Turk website.

2.1 Graphical Annotation Interface

In our annotation interface (Tratz and Phan, 2018), shown in Figure 1, words are displayed as nodes and dependencies are displayed as edges between them.[2] Turkers create dependency arcs by dragging and dropping word nodes. Dropping one node onto another forms a dependency arc between the two, with the dragged node as the dependent of the latter. While dragging, green circular dropzones appear to highlight possible attachment sites.

The tool is configured to have all words initially attached to the dummy root node. The *Submit HIT* button becomes operable only when there is exactly one word connected to the dummy root. Thus, annotators are required to reattach all but one of the words.

Annotation guidelines are accessible by clicking the *Instructions* button, which brings up a box with the instructions that can be opened into a separate window. Since many Turkers may be reluctant to read wordy guides, our instructions consist primarily of 55 small example trees.

2.2 Data

For our Mechanical Turk HITs, we construct a dataset consisting of 250 sentences from the Penn Treebank (Marcus et al., 1993) and 250 from The Westbury Lab Wikipedia corpus (Shaoul, 2010), each consisting of 10 to 15 alphanumeric tokens. We ignore Penn Treebank sentences that merely report changes in earnings figures, prices, etc., since these types of sentences are particularly frequent in the Penn Treebank and make for an undiverse (and, therefore, uninteresting) sample. With the Wikipedia data, we filter incomplete and ungrammatical sentences,[3] and sentences with offensive language, heavy use of foreign words, or esoteric technical content. We merge various date expressions (e.g., *March 15, 2000*) into single tokens since these elements can be recognized with high accuracy using regular expressions.

2.3 HIT configuration parameters

We require that Turkers who work on our HITs reside in the USA or Canada, have a 95% or higher approval rating, and have previously had at least 20 other HITs approved. We pay \$0.08[4] per completed assignment and request a total of 10 annotations per sentence (from 10 different workers).

2.4 Evaluation

For evaluation, we calculate both the percentage of words correctly attached (UAS: unlabeled attachment score) and the percentage of trees that

[1] We leave labeled dependency trees for future work, as labeling dependencies (e.g., 'subject', 'object') could be performed separately from the tree construction.

[2] Several aspects of the visual layout and styling of our tool are inspired by TREd (Pajas and Štěpánek, 2008).

[3] Many of these errors may be due to the overly aggressive nature of our sentence splitter.

[4] In practice, this proved to be rather low for the amount of time Turkers appear to have been spending, so we gave out bonuses of \$0.20 for most HIT assignments after all assignments were received.

Worker	Trees	Penn Treebank				Wikipedia			
		Trees	UAS	FTM	$\widetilde{\text{time}}$	Trees	UAS	FTM	$\widetilde{\text{time}}$
W1	177	90	0.921	0.500	53.5	87	0.935	0.552	51
W2	453	223	0.913	0.439	37	230	0.918	0.465	33
W3	499	249	0.906	0.454	44	250	0.907	0.428	41
W4	410	201	0.901	0.443	42	209	0.901	0.407	38
W5	412	194	0.840	0.211	40	218	0.865	0.261	36
W6	450	226	0.796	0.159	45.5	224	0.831	0.228	38.5
W7	411	207	0.774	0.077	54	204	0.792	0.127	47.5
W8	434	211	0.724	0.057	55	223	0.768	0.112	44
W9	119	61	0.724	0.115	34	58	0.708	0.138	35.5
W10	352	178	0.644	0.034	45.5	174	0.688	0.052	39
W11	197	107	0.500	0.000	111	90	0.518	0.000	94
W12	128	59	0.423	0.000	311	69	0.434	0.000	238
W13	379	185	0.228	0.000	48	194	0.245	0.000	46
A1	500	250	0.969	0.712	—	250	1.000	1.000	—

Table 1: Results for the 13 workers (W1–W13) who annotate 50 or more Penn Treebank trees, including the total number of trees annotated, unlabeled attachment scores (UAS), full tree match rate (FTM), and median time in seconds ($\widetilde{\text{time}}$) between accepting a HIT and submitting results. For reference, we also include scores for the primary author (A1).

fully match the reference (FTM: full tree match rate). In the case of the Penn Treebank sentences, the reference is the automatic dependency conversion; for the Wikipedia sentences, we use the primary author's annotation. A total of 112 Turkers participate; however, most only annotate 1 or 2 sentences, making it difficult to estimate their aptitude for this task. The 13 workers who annotated 50 or more sentence account for over 88% of the annotations received. The scores for these 13 most prolific annotators are presented in Table 1, along with the scores for the primary author (who is, ideally, representative of an expert annotator) included as well for comparison.

2.5 Results Discussion

We note a high degree of variation in the quality of the work of the different annotators. Four of the more prolific Turkers achieve attachment scores of 90% or higher on the Penn Treebank portion of the data, but others are unable to reach even 50% agreement. To examine how the Turkers' performance varies with time, we plot the change to their overall attachment scores as they perform annotations (see Figure 2). Several annotators, including *W6*, *W8*, *W10*, and *W11*, improve noticeably early on as they gain experience. A couple annotators (i.e., *W2* and *W7*) show slight decreases in their scores, which may be due to fatigue. Overall, there appears to be a very high degree of consistency over time for the individual Turkers.

For 72% of the Penn Treebank sentences, at least one annotator produces a dependency tree that fully matches the reference completely. Taking the Turker-provided tree that best matches the reference for each of the PTB sentences results in a set of trees with a 96.8% attachment score, 3257 of 3363 attachments agreeing. Examining the remaining 106 disagreements in more detail, we observe that approximately 13 are due to handling of business suffixes (e.g., Corp., Co.), at least 8 are due to errors in the reference, and 5 are related to quantifying adverbs preceding expressions with numbers (e.g., *about 8 %*). Many of these disagreements could be brought into alignment by tweaking the annotation guide and/or fixing bugs in the dependency conversion. The remaining errors fall into a wide variety of categories. A substantial portion are related to phenomena that are somewhat challenging to represent well with dependency parses, such as gapping, right node raising, and *it* extraposition.

In general, the results seem to suggest that the Wikipedia sentences may be slightly easier to parse, but, overall, the results are quite similar to those for the PTB sentences.

3 Related Work

To date, there have been very few efforts to crowdsource parsing and no efforts, to the best of our knowledge, to do so directly with a full parse tree editor like ours other than in small classroom studies like that of Gerdes (2013).

In what is the most closely related line of work, researchers build and deploy a Game with a Purpose (GWAP) (Von Ahn, 2006) called ZOM-

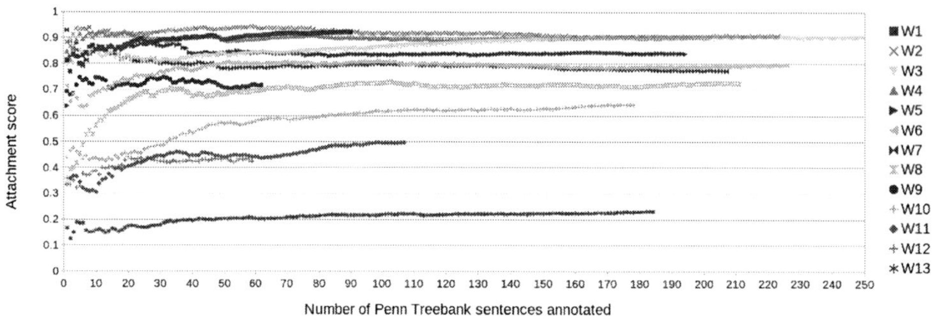

Figure 2: Overall unlabeled attachment score on Penn Treebank sentences for the 13 most prolific workers (W1–W13), calculated as each annotation is received. (Note: Workers do not annotate sentences in the same order.)

BILINGO in order to crowdsource a French treebank (Fort et al., 2014; Guillaume et al., 2016; Fort et al., 2017). ZOMBILINGO participants, who are all volunteers, work on one attachment decision at a time, using the metaphor that the governing word is devouring the child just as zombies seek out brains. The participants must complete a training phase for each dependency relation type that they work on, and they are unable to proceed to relations deemed more difficult until they have demonstrated some skill on less challenging dependency relations.

Another related effort is that of He et al. (2016), who, in an initial step toward human-in-the-loop parsing, crowdsource individual attachment annotations by asking annotators multiple choice questions automatically generated using parse trees produced by an existing parser. They are able to achieve some performance gains, including a 0.2 F1 improvement on their in-domain corpus (from 88.1 to 88.3) and a 0.6 F1 improvement on their out-of-domain corpus (from 82.2 to 82.8).

It is worth noting that there are a number of ethical concerns regarding the use of Mechanical Turk, and a variety of articles have been written on this subject. We refer the reader to a discussion of these issues by Fort et al. (2011).

4 Conclusion and Future Work

This paper details the first effort to crowdsource treebanking using Mechanical Turk or similar online crowdsourcing platform. Using our graphical web-based treebanking tool, we collect 10 dependency parse annotations for each of 500 sentences. Despite not requiring any training, several of the annotators achieve attachment scores at or above 90%. Although this may not be of sufficient quality to train a competitive English parser, it establishes a baseline for dependency tree annotation using workers who are presumably non-experts, demonstrating the potential value that non-experts can bring to parsing annotation projects. Moreover, treebanks with 90% attachment accuracy would still be useful for other languages, especially those with little or no annotated data. To this end, we plan to investigate whether our approach will result in comparable accuracy for other languages, which will likely require recruiting workers outside of Mechanical Turk.

We find that taking the best tree for each of the 250 Penn Treebank sentences results in a dataset that agrees with the Penn Treebank dependency conversion on 96.8% of attachments and agrees with the full dependency tree 72% of the time. Though unreasonable to assume that any such oracle exists, it may be possible to approach this level of accuracy by employing a multi-step approach in which workers review and judge the work of others, similar to the translation crowdsourcing efforts of Zaidan and Callison-Burch (2011). To facilitate research among the greater community into techniques for aggregating complex crowdsourced annotations, we provide our annotated dataset at `https://github.com/USArmyResearchLab/ARL_CrowdTree`.

Finally, we plan to integrate active learning algorithms that run while the Turkers are annotating. A *query by committee* (Seung et al., 1992) framework would be a natural choice—multiple different parsing models would learn from the submitted trees and the sentences provided to the annotators would be selected based upon the level of disagreement between the parsers.

References

Alena Böhmová, Jan Hajič, Eva Hajičová, and Barbora Hladká. 2003. The Prague Dependency Treebank. In Anne Abeillé, editor, *Treebanks: Building and Using Parsed Corpora*, pages 103–127. Springer Netherlands.

Karën Fort, Gilles Adda, and K Bretonnel Cohen. 2011. Amazon Mechanical Turk: Gold Mine or Coal Mine? *Computational Linguistics*, 37(2):413–420.

Karën Fort, Bruno Guillaume, and Hadrien Chastant. 2014. Creating Zombilingo, a Game With A Purpose for dependency syntax annotation. In *Proceedings of the First International Workshop on Gamification for Information Retrieval*, pages 2–6.

Karën Fort, Bruno Guillaume, and Nicolas Lefebvre. 2017. Who wants to play Zombie? A survey of the players on ZOMBILINGO. In *Proceedings of Games4NLP: Using Games and Gamification for Natural Language Processing*.

Kim Gerdes. 2013. Collaborative Dependency Annotation. In *Proceedings of the Second International Conference on Dependency Linguistics (DepLing 2013)*, pages 88–97.

Bruno Guillaume, Karen Fort, and Nicolas Lefebvre. 2016. Crowdsourcing Complex Language Resources: Playing to Annotate Dependency Syntax. In *Proceedings of the 26th International Conference on Computational Linguistics (COLING)*, pages 3041–3052.

Luheng He, Julian Michael, Mike Lewis, and Luke Zettlemoyer. 2016. Human-in-the-Loop Parsing. In *Proceedings of the 2016 Conference on Empirical Methods in Natural Language Processing (EMNLP 2016)*, pages 2337–2342.

Mitchell P. Marcus, Mary A. Marcinkiewicz, and Beatrice Santorini. 1993. Building a Large Annotated Corpus of English: The Penn Treebank. *Computational Linguistics*, 19(2):330.

Petr Pajas and Jan Štěpánek. 2008. Recent Advances in a Feature-Rich Framework for Treebank Annotation. In *Proceedings of the 22nd International Conference on Computational Linguistics*, pages 673–680. Association for Computational Linguistics.

H Sebastian Seung, Manfred Opper, and Haim Sompolinsky. 1992. Query by Committee. In *Proceedings of the fifth annual workshop on Computational learning theory*, pages 287–294.

Cyrus Shaoul. 2010. The Westbury Lab Wikipedia Corpus. *Edmonton, Alberta: University of Alberta.*

Stephen Tratz and Nhien Phan. 2018. A Web-based System for Crowd-in-the-Loop Dependency Treebanking. In *Proceedings of the Eleventh International Conference on Language Resources and Evaluation (LREC-2018)*, pages 2189–2193.

Luis Von Ahn. 2006. Games with a Purpose. *Computer*, 39(6):92–94.

Omar F Zaidan and Chris Callison-Burch. 2011. Crowdsourcing Translation: Professional Quality from Non-Professionals. In *Proceedings of the 49th Annual Meeting of the Association for Computational Linguistics: Human Language Technologies-Volume 1*, pages 1220–1229.

Word Familiarity Rate Estimation Using a Bayesian Linear Mixed Model

Masayuki Asahara
National Institute for Japanese Language and Linguistics, Japan
masayu-a at ninjal dot ac dot jp

Abstract

This paper presents research on word familiarity rate estimation using the 'Word List by Semantic Principles'. We collected rating information on 96,557 words in the 'Word List by Semantic Principles' via Yahoo! crowdsourcing. We asked 3,392 subject participants to use their introspection to rate the familiarity of words based on the five perspectives of 'KNOW', 'WRITE', 'READ', 'SPEAK', and 'LISTEN', and each word was rated by at least 16 subject participants. We used Bayesian linear mixed models to estimate the word familiarity rates. We also explored the ratings with the semantic labels used in the 'Word List by Semantic Principles'.

1 Introduction

Compiling a lexicon is difficult work. In the lexicography field, there are two main types of methodology that are utilized to compile lexicons. One is a corpus-based methodology, which supports the objectivity of the language resources and results. This methodology requires large-scale, balanced corpora to function, which do exist in several languages; for instance, there are several corpus databases for the Japanese language, such as the 'Balanced Corpus of Contemporary Written Japanese' (Maekawa et al., 2014), the 'Corpus of Spontaneous Japanese' (Maekawa et al., 2000) and the 'NINJAL Web Japanese Corpus' (Asahara et al., 2014). In contrast to the corpus-based lexicography, the intuition-based method is more rooted in the subjective perspective of the lexicographer. Nowadays, however, we can perform large-scale experiments that gather enough crowdsourced subjective perspectives to constitute objective linguistic data on individual words.

Generally, a lexicon covers several layers of linguistic features, such as pronunciation, morphological information, part-of-speech or word class, relevant syntactic phenomena, and semantic categories. In addition, the terms in a lexicon include additional features that are used in daily life. One such language resource in Japanese is the 'Word Familiarity Rate', which measures how familiar people are with a specific word by NTT[1](Amano and Kondo, 1999). However, this 'Word Familiarity Rate' experiment was completed more than twenty years ago, and it is therefore possible that the usage and register of words have changed in the intervening years.

In this study, we construct a word familiarity rate database using entries extracted from the 'Word List by Semantic Principles' (『分類語彙表』 Bunrui goihyo, hereafter WLSP) (Kokuritsu_Kokugo_Kenkyusho, 2004). We utilized crowdsourcing to perform a large-scale subjective experiment on 96,557 WLSP entries. We asked the subject participants to rate the familiarity of words along five perspectives: KNOW, WRITE, READ, SPEAK, and LISTEN. The quality of results gathered by crowdsourcing may be lower than that of results collected in a controlled experiment; however, the cost of constructing a crowdsourced study is lower than the cost of conducting an experiment. We utilized a Bayesian linear mixed model (Sorensen et al., 2016) to alleviate noise in the data.

Our work makes the following contributions to the literature:

- We compiled a word familiarity rate database for thesaurus entries.
- We used crowdsourcing via human subject participants to explore word ratings.
- We introduced a Bayesian linear mixed model to this type of rate modelling.

[1]Nippon Telegraph and Telephone Corporation.

Proceedings of the First Workshop on Aggregating and Analysing Crowdsourced Annotations for NLP, pages 6–14
Hong Kong, China, November 3, 2019. ©2019 Association for Computational Linguistics
https://doi.org/10.18653/v1/P17

Table 1: Example Entry from the 'Word List by Semantic Principles'

「昨年」 'Last Year': 1.1642			
Syntactic Category	Semantic Category		
	Top Level	Second Level	Finest Level
体 Nominal Word 1.	関係 Relation .1	時間 Time .16	過去 Past Time .1642

- The word list was taken from the surface forms of WLSP. This enabled us to connect word familiarity rates with the semantic categories in a thesaurus. Kondo et al. (2018) produced a correspondence table between WLSP and UniDic (a lexicon with morphological information). The morphological analyser MeCab enabled us to automatically annotate the familiarity rates using these resources.
- The preceding work introduced the contrast between character-based (WRITE, READ) and voice-based (SPEAK, LISTEN) perspectives. We contributed to the literature by also introducing a new contrast between production (WRITE, SPEAK) and reception (READ, LISTEN) perspectives.

The remainder of this paper is organised as follows. Section 2 presents related work on the 'Word List by Semantic Principles' and the 'Word Familiarity Rate' in Japanese. Section 3 displays the methodology that we used to develop the word familiarity ratings, namely, crowdsourcing and a Bayesian linear mixed model. Section 4 evaluates the results, and Section 5 presents a conclusion and discusses future research.

2 Related Work

2.1 'Word List by Semantic Principles'

The 'Word List by Semantic Principles' (分類語彙表, WLSP) is one of the major thesauri for contemporary Japanese. The first version of the WLSP was released in 1964 by Kokuritsu Kokugo Kenkyusho (Kokuritsu_Kokugo_Kenkyusho, 1964), and a newer, expanded version was published in 2004 (Kokuritsu_Kokugo_Kenkyusho, 2004). Its comma separated value (CSV) file of the expanded version can be used for research purposes.[2]

[2] 200,000 yen (+ tax) for commercial use.

The data include more than 90,000 words with four syntactic categories (nominal word, verbal word, modifer word, and other) and several hierarchical semantic levels. The categories are indicated with a one integer digit to the left of a radix point and with four fractional digits to the right of the radix point. Table 1 shows an example of the word '昨年 (Last Year)', which is assigned a value of 1.1642. Here, the first '1' presents the syntactic part, which is referred to as the 'Nominal Word', while '1642' presents the hierarchical semantic part, as follows: the first digit, '.1', refers to the top-level semantic category 'Relation'; the two digits '.16' refer to the second-level semantic category 'Time'; and the four digits '.1642' refer to the finest-grained semantic category 'Past Time'. These five digits are therefore referred to as the 'WLSP number'. The syntactic categories are 1. Nominal Word, 2. Verbal Word, 3. Modifier Word, and 4. Other (e.g. Conjunction, Interjection, Greeting).

We used all the words as the target words to be annotated for familiarity rates.

2.2 Word Familiarity Rate in Japanese

Preceding work used two methods to estimate the word familiarity ratings: a word frequency-based (objective) and a cognitive experiment-based (subjective) method. The *Nihongo-no goitokusei database* (Amano and Kondo, 1999) includes both objective and subjective data for word familiarity ratings. The data were constructed from 14 years of *Asahi Shinbun* newspaper articles, from 1985 to 1998. They used a morphological analyser, Sumomo, to analyse the articles and split the sentences into words.

The subjective data are cognitive experiment-based. The 40 participants rated word familiarity of three types of stimuli: character-based, voice-based, and both. The participants were chosen based on 'Hyakurakan' (百羅漢), – a Japanese proficiency test – to control their linguistic competence. The rating score is an integer from 1 (lowest) to 7 (highest), and the number of target entries is 88,569 of character and voice-based stimuli, from 69,084 words. The data gathering was held from September 1995 to July 1996 in the NTT institute. Even though the rating environment was controlled, the estimation of the word familiarity was based on the average of ratings by participants. More sophisticated statistical analysis should be utilised for reducing the subject participant biases.

3 Methodology

3.1 Design

In this section, we present our methodology for constructing a word familiarity rate lexicon at low cost. The word list constitutes 96,557 words taken from the WLSP. We did not prepare any voice data (oral pronunciations) for the lexical entries, but we did cover speech and hearing as two of the following five perspectives:

KNOW: how much do you know about the target word?

WRITE: how often do you write the word?

READ: how often do you read the word?

SPEAK: how often do you speak the word?

LISTEN: how often do you listen to the word?

In this design, we split the judgements between character-based (WRITE and READ) and voice-based (SPEAK and LISTEN) judgements and between production (WRITE and SPEAK) and reception (READ and LISTEN) judgements. The participants gave five ratings for each factor, ranging from 5 (well known/often used) to 1 (little known/rarely used).

The rating data were collected not in person but on a crowdsourcing platform. We used 'Yahoo! crowdsourcing'; 3,392 participants judged the word familiarity rates. The participants checked a stimulus word and answered rating scores for KNOW, WRITE, READ, SPEAK, and READ; at least 16 answers were collected for each word. The data were gathered on November, 2018. The data collection, which cost 1,455,494 yen, was completed within two weeks.

3.2 Model

The collected rating data is biased due to the use of the particular subject participants, which necessitates that statistical methods should be used to resolve the biases. We used a Bayesian linear mixed model to measure the ratings. The graphical model used to estimate the ratings is shown in Figure 3: N_{word} is the number of words, and N_{subj} is the number of participants; Index $i : 1 \dots N_{word}$ is the index of words, and index $j : 1 \dots N_{subj}$ is the index of participants; and $y^{(i)(j)}$ is the rating of KNOW, WRITE, READ, SPEAK, LISTEN, in which y is generated by a Normal distribution with $\mu^{(i)(j)}$ and σ, as follows:

$$y^{(i)(j)} \sim Normal(\mu^{(i)(j)}, \sigma).$$

Here, the σ is a hyper-parameter of the standard deviation, and $\mu^{(i)(j)}$ is a linear formula of slopes $\gamma^{(i)}_{subj}$, slopes $\gamma^{(i)}_{word}$ and an intercept α:

$$\mu^{(i)(j)} = \alpha + \gamma^{(i)}_{word} + \gamma^{(j)}_{subj}.$$

The slopes are modelled by a Normal distribution with the hyper-parameters of μ_{word}, σ_{word}, μ_{subj}, σ_{subj} (means and standard deviations):

$$\gamma^{(i)}_{word} \sim Normal(\mu_{word}, \sigma_{word}),$$

$$\gamma^{(j)}_{subj} \sim Normal(\mu_{subj}, \sigma_{subj}).$$

The word familiarity rates are composed by $\gamma^{(i)}_{word}$. On the other hand, the biases of subject participants are modelled by $\gamma^{(j)}_{subj}$. We set the means μ_{word} and μ_{subj} as 0.0 to make the average 0.0; we also set the standard deviations σ_{word} and σ_{subj} as 1.0. We used R and Stan to model the data. We set an iteration at 5,000 $\times$ 4 chains with an initial warm-up of 100 iterations.

4 Data Analysis

This section describes the qualitative evaluation of the estimated word familiarity rate data. To evaluate the data, we first reviewed the distribution of the five perspectives and the biases of the subject participants. Second, we confirmed the top and bottom 10 words of the estimated values. Third, we also reviewed the top and bottom 10 categories by the WLSP's second semantic category for the estimated values.

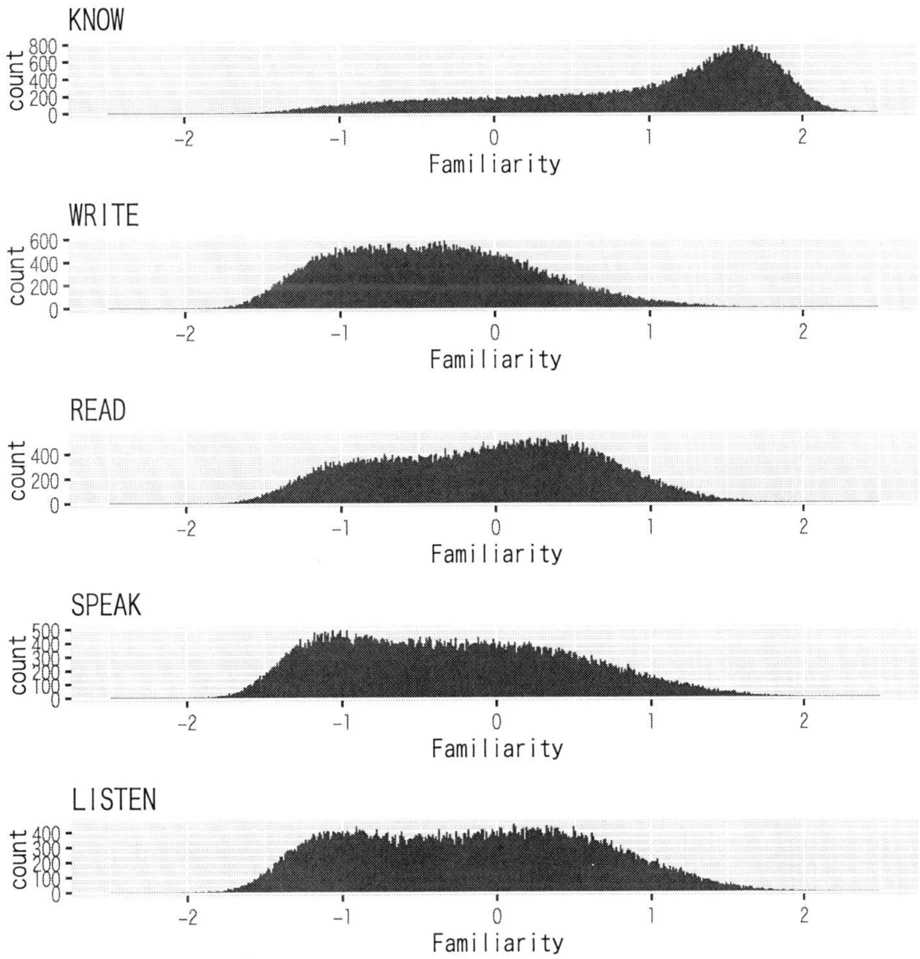

Figure 1: Estimated Familiarities ($\gamma_{word}^{(i)}$): The Distribution of the Five Perspectives

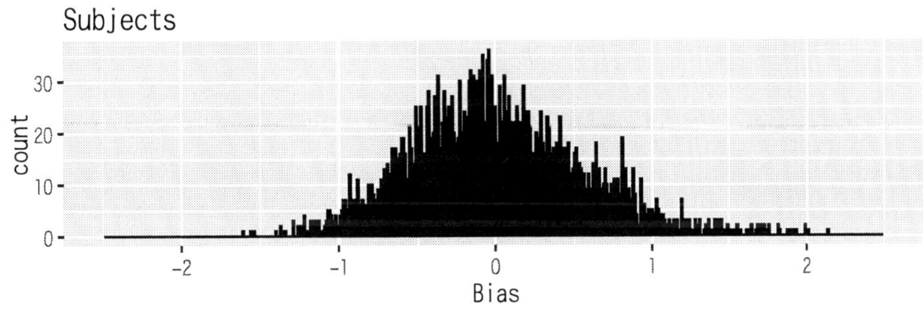

Figure 2: Estimated Biases for the Subject Participants ($\gamma_{subj}^{(j)}$)

4.1 Distributions

Figure 1 displays the histogram of the estimated familiarities. The x-axis specifies the word famil-

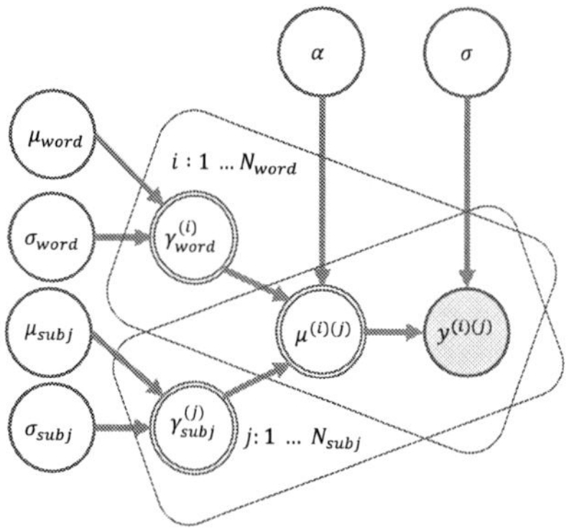

$$\gamma_{word}^{(i)} \sim Normal(\mu_{word}, \sigma_{word})$$
$$\gamma_{subj}^{(j)} \sim Normal(\mu_{subj}, \sigma_{subj})$$

$$\mu^{(i)(j)} = \alpha + \gamma_{word}^{(i)} + \gamma_{subj}^{(j)}$$
$$y^{(i)(j)} \sim Normal(\mu^{(i)(j)}, \sigma)$$

Figure 3: Graphical model for the Ratings

iarity rating $\gamma_{word}^{(i)}$, and the y-axis specifies the frequencies. The five perspectives are distinguished in the histogram with different colours. As illustrated in Figure 1, KNOW has a higher familiarity rating than the other perspectives, since it is the most fundamental perspective. The character-based perspectives (WRITE and READ) had lower familiarity ratings than the voice-based perspectives (SPEAK and LISTEN). Furthermore, the production perspectives (WRITE and SPEAK) had lower familiarity ratings than the reception perspectives (READ and LISTEN).

Figure 2 displays the histogram of the estimated subject participant biases. The x-axis specifies the estimated subject participant biases $\gamma_{subj}^{(j)}$, and the y-axis specifies the frequencies. The subject participant biases are modelled with standard normal distributions. We should introduce other distributions for the biases in our future work. We did attempt to use other distributions in the model; however, only the standard normal distribution converged. In future work, we will increase the amount of rating data and again attempt to use other distributions.

4.2 Evaluation by Words

In this section, we describe the top (KNOWN) and bottom (UNKNOWN) 10 words for several perspectives.

4.2.1 Known vs. Unknown

First, we reviewed KNOW, which is the most fundamental perspective.

Tables 2 and 3 display the top 10 known and unknown words for the perspective KNOW, respec-

Table 2: The Top 10 Known Words (KNOW)

Words		KNOW
全員	all	2.44
恋人	lover	2.44
翌朝（よくあさ）	next morning	2.44
退社する	leave the office	2.38
再会	reunion	2.38
本社	headquarters	2.38
入社	enter a company	2.37
人見知りする	timid	2.36
持ち帰る	take away	2.36
ストロー	straw	2.36

Table 3: The Top 10 Unknown Words

Words		KNOW
うずみひ	embeded gutter	-1.86
玉章（たまずさ）	letter	-1.86
御稜威（みいつ）	authority	-1.85
繞（にょう）	kanji radical	-1.85
鞅掌（おうしょう）する	being busy with	-1.84
スフ	staple fibre	-1.82
驍名	valor	-1.79
笈摺（おいずり）	sleeveless overgarment worn by pilgrims	-1.79
宇内（うだい）	the whole world	-1.76
賢察	hypothesise	-1.75

tively. The known words are ones that tend to be used in daily social life, while the unknown words are never or rarely used in Japan. Though we also analysed the other perspectives {WRITE, READ, SPEAK, LISTEN}, we omitted tables for the remaining four perspectives due to the limited space.

4.2.2 Character-based vs. Voice-based

Next, we surveyed the difference between the character-based (WRITE/READ) and voice-based (SPEAK/LISTEN) results by evaluating the values

Table 4: Character-based Biased Words

Words		Ch-Vo
上記	the abovementioned	3.88
追伸	postscript	2.65
前述する	mentioned earlier	2.42
後述	mention later	2.35
記	description	2.30
前略	dispensing with the preliminaries	2.29
在中	enclosed	2.18
アンパサンド [&]	ampersand	2.17
句読点	punctuation	2.12
下記	the undermentioned	2.00

Ch-Vo: WRITE + READ - SPEAK - LISTEN

Table 5: Voice-based Biased Words

Words		Ch-Vo
レジ袋	shopping bag	-3.07
先っちょ	tip	-2.65
ちょろまかす	embezzle	-2.59
バイバイ	bye bye	-2.59
ヨーグルト	yoghurt	-2.52
ドライヤー	dryer	-2.47
まんま [その〜]	as it is	-2.46
それではまた	see you again	-2.42
鼻水	mucus	-2.42
どっこいしょ	oof!	-2.41

Ch-Vo: WRITE + READ - SPEAK - LISTEN

for (WRITE + READ - SPEAK - LISTEN). The difference between character-based (WRITE and READ) and voice-based (SPEAK and LISTEN) stimuli can be observed in the '*Nihongo no goi tokusei*' database. Here, if the value is positive, the word tends to be used in written language. If the value is negative, the word tends to be used in spoken language.

Table 4 shows the positively-valued examples. These words tend to be used in written documents or letters. Punctuation-related words 'アンパサンド (ampersand)' and '句読点 (punctuation)' also appeared in the top 10 words. Table 5 shows the negatively-valued examples. These words tend to be used in conversations in daily life. The greeting 'バイバイ (bye bye)' and the interjection 'どっこいしょ (oof!)' are also observed.

4.2.3 Production vs. Reception

We surveyed the difference between the production (WRITE/SPEAK) and reception (READ/LISTEN) results and evaluated the (WRITE + SPEAK - READ - LISTEN) values. This approach is unique because no existing research has evaluated these perspectives.

The difference between production and reception thus seems to reflect whether or not the word is used in both mass media and in normal speech. Table 6 shows the production biased words, which tend to be technical terms. Some of the subject participants' work histories (e.g. in the medical or music fields) explain certain words in Table 6, such as '毛管 (capillary tube)' and '絆創膏 (adhesive tape)' or traditional music '吟詠する (sing a song)'. Table 7 shows the reception biased words, and the negative words ('殺害 (murder)' and '書類送検 (filling charges)') are confirmed. The word '西郷隆盛 (Takamori Saigo)' also appears as a reception biased word in Table 6, which is the main character in a TV drama.

Table 6: Production Biased Words

Words		P-R
毛管	capillary tube	0.76
物心（ぶっしん）	matterand mind	0.73
消却する	erase	0.73
絆創膏	adhesive tape	0.72
ふたとせ	two years	0.71
揚げなべ	deep fryers	0.71
吟詠する	sing a song	0.71
だるい	feel weary	0.69
上辺（うわべ）	outward appearance	0.68
幽寂	sequestered	0.66

P-R: WRITE + SPEAK - READ - LISTEN

Table 7: Reception Biased Words

Word		P-R
送検する	commit someone to trial	-2.93
右翼	right wing	-2.71
書類送検	filing charges	-2.69
巡業する	take a provincial tour	-2.59
西郷隆盛	Takamori Saigo	-2.52
殺害（さつがい・せつがい）	murder	-2.52
革命児	revolutionary	-2.48
護衛する	guard	-2.47
識者	well-informed people	-2.42
再審	retrial	-2.41

P-R: WRITE + SPEAK - READ - LISTEN

4.3 Evaluation by WLSP categories

This section presents our evaluation of the WLSP categories. We evaluated the results using the second level of the semantic category in the WLSP, which includes two fractional digits to the right of the radix point (as explained in section 2.1). We also present the most and least familiar words in the same WLSP categories.

Table 8: The Top 10 Known Categories

	Category		KNOW
3.53	相-自然-生物	Modifier-Nature-Creature	1.41
3.17	相-関係-空間	Modifier-Relation-Space	1.41
2.10	用-関係-真偽	Verb-Relation-Truth	1.35
3.56	相-自然-身体	Modifier-Nature-Body	1.34
2.56	用-自然-身体	Verb-Nature-Body	1.32
2.14	用-関係-力	Verb-Relation-Power	1.32
3.35	相-活動-交わり	Relation-Action-Inter Course	1.32
4.32	他–呼び掛け	Other-Vocative	1.31
4.31	他–判断	Other-Judgement	1.29
3.57	相-自然-生命	Modifier-Nature-Life	1.26

Table 9: The Top 10 Unknown Categories

	Category		KNOW
3.52	相-自然-天地	Modifier-Nature-World	0.13
1.54	体-自然-植物	Noun-Nature-Botanical	0.40
1.55	体-自然-動物	Noun-Nature-Animal	0.64
1.31	体-活動-言語	Noun-Action-Language	0.66
1.23	体-主体-人物	Noun-Subject-Person	0.67
1.42	体-生産物-衣料	Noun-Product-Garments	0.68
1.52	体-自然-天地	Noun-Nature-World	0.70
1.32	体-活動-芸術	Noun-Action-Art	0.71
4.50	他-動物の鳴き声	Other-Animal Call	0.72
1.51	体-自然-物質	Noun-Nature-Material	0.76

4.3.1 Known vs. Unknown

Tables 8 and 9 display the top 10 known and unknown word categories based on the perspective KNOW, respectively. As illustrated in Tables 8 and 9, the known words tend to be modifiers or verbs, while the unknown words tend to be nouns. The most well-known category is 3.53 (相-自然-生物: Modifier-Nature-Creature), which includes gender-related words such as '女性的 (feminine)' (KNOW=1.81) and '男性的 (masculine)' (1.71). The least known category is 3.52 (相-自然-天地: Modifier-Nature-World), which includes rarely used words such as '蕭条 (bleak)' (-1.46) and '巍巍 (big and high)' (-1.35).

4.3.2 Character-based vs. Voice-based

Figures 10 and 11 display the results for the character-based biased and voice-based biased categories, respectively. As shown in these tables, the nominal action and subject categories tend to be character-based biased, whereas the vocative, interjection, modifiers, and animal call categories tend to be voice-based biased. The highest-valued character-based category is 1.31 (体-活動-言語: Noun-Action-Language), which includes epistolary words such as '上記 (aforementioned)' (WRITE+READ-SPEAK-LISTEN=3.87) and '追伸 (p.s.)' (2.65). The lowest valued voice-based biased category is 4.32 (他-呼びかけ: Other-Vocative), which includes 'もしもし (hello on phone)' (-1.75).

Table 10: Character-based Biased Categories

	Category		Ch-Vo
1.31	体-活動-言語	Noun-Action-Language	0.13
1.32	体-活動-芸術	Noun-Action-Art	0.11
1.25	体-主体-公私	Noun-Subject-Public Private	0.11
1.23	体-主体-人物	Noun-Subject-Person	0.10
1.27	体-主体-機関	Noun-Subject-Organisation	0.10
1.52	体-自然-天地	Noun-Nature-World	0.09
1.36	体-活動-待遇	Noun-Action-Treatment	0.08
2.31	用-活動-言語	Verb-Action-Language	0.07
1.53	体-自然-生物	Noun-Nature-Creature	0.07
3.52	相-自然-天地	Modifier-Nature-World	0.07

Ch-Vo: WRITE + READ - SPEAK - LISTEN

Table 11: Voice-based Biased Categories

	Category		Ch-Vo
4.32	他–呼び掛け	Other-Vocative	-0.59
4.30	他–感動	Other-Interjection	-0.53
3.56	相-自然-身体	Modifier-Nature-Body	-0.44
2.56	用-自然-身体	Verb-Nature-Body	-0.43
3.51	相-自然-物質	Modifier-Nature-Material	-0.42
3.18	相-関係-形	Modifier-Relation-Form	-0.33
3.50	相-自然-自然	Modifier-Nature-Nature	-0.30
3.57	相-自然-生命	Modifier-Nature-Creature	-0.29
4.50	他-動物の鳴き声	Other-Animal Call	-0.29
1.43	体-生産物-食料	Noun-Product-Food	-0.28

Ch-Vo: WRITE + READ - SPEAK - LISTEN

4.3.3 Production vs. Reception

Tables 12 and 13 display the results for the production biased and reception biased categories, respectively. Generally, the reception values (READ, LISTEN) tend to be larger than the production values (WRITE, SPEAK). Therefore, the

Table 12: Production Biased Categories

Category			P-R
4.50	他-動物の鳴き声	Other-Animal Call	-0.26
2.10	用-関係-真偽	Verb-Relation-Truth	-0.27
4.30	他-感動	Other-Interjection	-0.29
1.54	体-自然-植物	Noun-Nature-Botanical	-0.30
4.32	他-呼び掛け	Other-Vocative	-0.30
3.52	相-自然-天地	Modifier-Nature-World	-0.32
4.11	他-接続	Other-Conjunction	-0.35
1.42	体-生産物-衣料	Noun-Product-Garments	-0.35
1.55	体-自然-動物	Noun-Nature-Animal	-0.35
4.31	他-判断	Other-Judgement	-0.36

P-R: WRITE + SPEAK - READ - LISTEN

Table 13: Reception Biased Categories

Category			P-R
1.27	体-主体-機関	Noun-Subject-Organization	-0.62
1.36	体-活動-待遇	Noun-Action-Treatment	-0.56
1.35	体-活動-交わり	Noun-Action-Intercourse	-0.55
1.53	体-自然-生物	Noun-Nature-Creature	-0.54
3.17	相-関係-空間	Modifier-Relation-Space	-0.54
1.24	体-主体-成員	Noun-Subject-Member	-0.54
2.35	用-活動-交わり	Verb-Action-Inter Course	-0.53
2.36	用-活動-待遇	Verb-Action-Treatment	-0.53
2.34	用-活動-行為	Verb-Action-Behaviour	-0.52
3.14	相-関係-力	Verb-Relation-Power	-0.52

P-R: WRITE + SPEAK - READ - LISTEN

values for Pro-Rec (WRITE + SPEAK - READ - LISTEN) become negative, even for the production biased categories. The syntactic categories (excluding nouns, verbs, and modifiers) are production biased such as the animal call, interjection, vocative, and conjunction categories. The other production biased category is 4.50 (他-動物の鳴き声: Other-Animal Call), which includes words such as 'げろげろ (croak)' (WRITE+SPEAK-READ-LISTEN=0.45) and 'かーかー (croak)' (0.23). The reception biased words refer to the vocabulary used on the news or in TV show such as nominal organisation, treatment, or intercourse. The reception biased category with the highest ranking is 1.27 (体-主体-機関: Noun-Subject-Organization), which includes words such as '厚生労働省 (Ministry of Health, Labour, and Welfare)' (-2.23) and '金融庁 (Financial Services Agency)' (-2.18).

4.4 Discussions

In this paper, we presented the word familiarity rating tendencies based on a crowdsourced study. The character-based (WRITE and READ) /voice-based (SPEAK and LISTEN) contrasting results confirm the findings in *Nihongo no goi tokusei*; however, in our data, we uniquely observe the contrast between the production and reception categories.

However, we still face the issue of normalising the ratings. This study ' s proposed method, in which the mean and standard deviation are set to 0.0 and 1.0, respectively, is sufficient when rating relative values or when arranging ratings in a certain order. We also calculated the ratings with $\gamma^{(i)}_{word} + \mu_{subj} + \alpha$; with this calculation, the ratings can be ranged from 1.0 to 5.0, excluding outliers. Though the normalization of ratings should be determined by the rating method used, calculating the value $\gamma^{(i)}_{word}$ is sufficient for most uses.

5 Conclusions

We have presented a Japanese word familiarity rate database for entries in the WLSP. To do so, we used crowdsourcing to explore the word familiarity ratings in terms of five perspectives: KNOW, WRITE, READ, SPEAK, and LISTEN. A Bayesian linear mixed model was utilised to estimate the ratings. The data [3] and code[4] are publicly available. Our future work on this topic is as follows. In this paper, we modelled the word familiarity rates and the subject participant biases with the standard normal distribution. While we did attempt to model the rates and biases with other distributions, the MCMC estimation did not converge. In the future, we hope to perform the survey on a yearly basis (to enlarge the data size) in order to model other distributions. We will also enhance the target word list to include UniDic entries for content words. In addition, we plan to create a morphological analyser, which will extract the word familiarity rates.

Acknowledgments

This work was supported by JSPS KAKENHI Grants Number 17H00917, 18H05521, 18K18519, 19K00591, 19K00655 and a project of the Center for Corpus Development, NINJAL.

[3] https://cradle.ninjal.ac.jp/

[4] https://github.com/masayu-a/WLSP-familiarity

References

Shigeaki Amano and Tadahisa Kondo, editors. 1999. *Nihongo no goi tokusei (Lexical properties of Japanese)*. Sanseido, Tokyo.

Masayuki Asahara, Kikuo Maekawa, Mizuho Imada, Sachi Kato, and Hikari Konishi. 2014. Archiving and analysing techniques of the ultra-large-scale web-based corpus project of ninjal, japan. *Alexandria*, 1–2:129–148.

Kokuritsu_Kokugo_Kenkyusho. 1964. *Bunrui goihyo (Word List by Sementic Principles)*. Shuei Shuppan, Tokyo.

Kokuritsu_Kokugo_Kenkyusho. 2004. *Bunrui goihyo zouho kaitei-ban (Word List by Sementic Principles, Revised and Enlarged Edition)*. Dainippon Tosho, Tokyo.

Asuko Kondo, Makiro Tanaka, and Masayuki Asahara. 2018. Alignment table between unidic and 'word list by semantic principles'. In *Proceedings of The Eighth Conference of Japanese Association for Digital Humanities (JADH2018)*, pages 125–128.

Kikuo Maekawa, Hanae Koiso, Sadaoki Furui, and Hitoshi Isahara. 2000. Spontaneous speech corpus of japanese. In *Proceedings of LREC-2000, (Second International Conference on Language Resources and Evaluation)*, volume 2, pages 947–952.

Kikuo Maekawa, Makoto Yamazaki, Toshinobu Ogiso, Takehiko Maruyama, Hideki Ogura, Wakako Kashino, Hanae Koiso, Masaya Yamaguchi, Makiro Tanaka, and Yasuharu Den. 2014. Balanced corpus of contemporary written japanese. *Language Resources and Evaluation*, 48(2):345–371.

Tanner Sorensen, Sven Hohenstein, and Shravan Vasishth. 2016. Bayesian linear mixed models using stan: A tutorial for psychologists, linguists, and cognitive scientists. *Quantitative Methods for Psychology*, 12(3):175–200.

Leveraging syntactic parsing to improve event annotation matching

Camiel Colruyt, Orphée De Clercq, Véronique Hoste
LT[3], Language and Translation Technology Team
Ghent University
Groot-Brittanniëlaan 45, 9000 Ghent, Belgium
firstname.lastname@ugent.be

Abstract

Detecting event mentions is the first step in event extraction from text and annotating them is a notoriously difficult task. Evaluating annotator consistency is crucial when building datasets for mention detection. When event mentions are allowed to cover many tokens, annotators may disagree on their span, which means that overlapping annotations may then refer to the same event or to different events. This paper explores different fuzzy matching functions which aim to resolve this ambiguity. The functions extract the sets of syntactic heads present in the annotations, use the Dice coefficient to measure the similarity between sets and return a judgment based on a given threshold. The functions are tested against the judgments of a human evaluator and a comparison is made between sets of tokens and sets of syntactic heads. The best-performing function is a head-based function that is found to agree with the human evaluator in 89% of cases.

1 Introduction

The extraction of event descriptions from text has been the subject of many research efforts in the last decades (Vossen, 2016; Peng et al., 2015; Aguilar et al., 2014). Downstream tasks such as event coreference have also been studied (Lu and Ng, 2018, 2017; Araki and Mitamura, 2015). More specifically, *event mention extraction* refers to the task of identifying spans in the text that mention certain real-world events, as well as extracting given features of that mention. For example, the sentence "A car bomb exploded in central Baghdad", according to the ACE guidelines (noa, 2008), contains a mention of an event of the type *Conflict.Attack*.

The difficulties of annotating events have been extensively discussed. Conceptually, events are difficult to define, as they are open to interpretation and may be worded in idiosyncratic ways (Vossen et al., 2018). Poor recall – i.e., human annotators not consistently recognising that events occur – is an acknowledged issue in event mention studies (Mitamura et al., 2015; Inel and Aroyo, 2019). Many datasets work with a fixed set of labels, representing the different semantic categories an event mention can belong to, but the choice of labels can be ambiguous. The reliability of such datasets has therefore been questioned (Vossen et al., 2018). Despite this ambiguity, annotation projects usually assume that there is a ground truth to event extraction, and trust a small number of annotators to discover it. Crowdsourcing event annotation can relax the search for a ground truth and reflect the ambiguity of the task more closely, as well as provide an implicit consistency-checking mechanism. (Inel and Aroyo, 2019), for instance, use crowdsourcing to validate and extend the annotations of select event and time datasets.

Another issue is that, as different research projects design conceptualizations geared to specific tasks, the resulting data sets are specialized to a certain degree: they over- or underrepresent certain genres event types. Models trained on this data can perform well within that range but transfer poorly to work with uncurated data in a real world context (Araki and Mitamura, 2018). This relationship between task, dataset and performance has been examined in e.g. Grishman (2010).

In many event annotation schemas (RED (O'Gorman et al., 2016), ACE (Peng et al., 2016), ECB+ (Cybulska and Vossen, 2014), MEANTIME (Minard et al., 2016)), event mention detection relies on the identification of a single-token lexical trigger for the event. In "A car bomb exploded in central Baghdad", the token *exploded* is annotated as the trigger (noa, 2008). The 2014 Knowledge Base Population (KBP) track of the Text Analysis Conference (TAC) introduced Event

Proceedings of the First Workshop on Aggregating and Analysing Crowdsourced Annotations for NLP, pages 15–23
Hong Kong, China, November 3, 2019. ©2019 Association for Computational Linguistics
https://doi.org/10.18653/v1/P17

Nuggets, an event description that allows tagging multiple tokens as the event trigger. Multi-token triggers allow annotators to more easily navigate cases in which multiple words could be chosen as a trigger, e.g. "hold a meeting", "serve a sentence", and they can be continuous or discontinuous (Mitamura et al., 2015).

In this paper event triggers are further generalized to comprise entire clauses, encompassing all arguments to the event, in order to alleviate the same type of issues we found when annotating Dutch news text (see Section 3 for a description of this project). However, using expanded triggers introduces the possibility that annotators may identify the same *events* while disagreeing on the exact *span* of the event mentions, either through error or a different interpretation of the mention's scope. It is therefore important to monitor the quality and consistency of annotations. This is all the more true given the expensive and time-consuming nature of annotation. Inter-annotator agreement studies must be conducted carefully to gauge how human annotators interpret and apply certain guidelines.

In a consistency study, F-score is measured by determining in how far different annotators recognize the same event mentions in a text. When annotations from both annotators cover the same span, this is trivial. However, when annotators annotate the same event but mark different spans, a fuzzy matching mechanism is necessary to recognize that both annotations refer to the same event. In this paper, we explore such fuzzy matching methods and compare two different methods: matching the similarity between token sets as done in previous work (Liu et al., 2015), versus relying on syntactic head sets which are obtained through parsing. We find that using heads leads to results that lie closer to the judgment of a human evaluator.

The remainder of this paper is organized as follows: in Section 2 previous research on evaluating event mention annotations is described. Section 3 introduces the event dataset and annotation procedure. Section 4 explains the methodology for matching annotation pairs and in Section 5, the results are described. Section 6 concludes this paper and offers prospects for future work.

2 Related work

Event recognition was introducted as a task in the ACE program in 2004. Event mention recall was not evaluated directly; rather, scoring happened on the level of *events* rather than *event mentions* (such that one event is a bucket of multiple mentions referring to the same event). A mapping between gold mentions and system output mentions was a prerequisite for scoring (Doddington et al., 2004). The same is true for the Event Mention Detection (VMD) task in ACE 2005 (National Institute of Standards and Technology, 2005). The ACE 2005 corpus thereafter became widely used in event detection studies. Because triggers consist of single-word tokens, testing recall is straightforward. Li et al. (2013) and Li et al. (2014), for instance, treat matches as correct if their offsets (span) and event subtype match exactly. F1 is used to score performance overall.

Event nugget detection, and with it event triggers that consist of more than one word, were introduced as a task in the TAC KBP track in 2014. Liu et al. (2015) proposes a method to evaluate nugget recall which enables fuzzy matching for annotations with non-perfectly-overlapping spans. In this work the Dice coefficient is used to measure the set similarity between the tokens covered by each annotation, which turns out to be the same as F1 score. System mentions are mapped to gold standard mentions by selecting the gold-system pair with the highest Dice coefficient score. An overall matching score is produced by considering other features of the event annotation. Mitamura et al. (2015) uses this method to assess the consistency of annotation in the 2014 TAC KBP corpus. This paper uses the same idea and takes the Dice coefficient to map annotations from different annotators, but applies it to the sets of heads of mentions. Additionally, Dice-based methods are applied to token sets to examine the advantages of using heads over tokens. However, the triggers in event nuggets still mostly consist of single tokens (Mitamura et al., 2015) and multi-token triggers are kept minimally short. In our task, event mentions span several tokens by default, making a straightforward comparison difficult.

3 Dataset and annotations

In this paper we report on the inter-annotator agreement (IAA) study of an event annotation task carried out in the framework of the #NewsDNA project, a large interdisciplinary research project on news diversity. To allow for automatic Dutch event extraction, training data is required and the objective is to annotate over 1,500 news articles coming from major Flemish publishers. In a first phase, 34 articles were annotated by four linguists to allow for the IAA study. For this paper, 4 additional articles were annotated and used to evaluate annotation matching methods.

The articles were annotated with information on events, entities and IPTC media topics[1]. Our event annotations are structurally similar to ACE/ERE events. The spans are marked and augmented with information on arguments, type and subtype (following a typology close to that of ACE/ERE), realis properties (polarity, tense and modality) and prominence (whether the event is a main event of an article or a background event). As mentioned before, the focus of this paper lies on the annotation of event mention spans, which can comprise entire verbal clauses or nominal constructions. Figure 1 shows an example of a fully-annotated event mention from the IAA set carried out in the WebAnno annotation tool (Yimam et al., 2014).

While annotation guidelines were devised describing the constraints of annotation as closely as possible, there is a large gray area in which annotators may interpret event span boundaries differently. For instance, in Table 1, examples 1 and 2 show cases where annotators disagreed on including descriptive clauses in the event mention. Matching annotations may also diverge due to annotation errors; in example 3, a punctuation mark was annotated by mistake. Consequently, matching annotations with different spans occur frequently in the IAA set. When we say two annotations *match*, we mean they intend to mark the same *mention* of the event in the text. (This differs from coreference, which aims to match different *mentions* that refer to the same event.) Contrasting with this, there are cases of overlapping annotations which do *not* refer to the same event, as in Table 2.

In order to conduct an IAA study, it is necessary to match the annotation of different annotators correctly. Such a matching function must mimic human judgment in finding that the span pairs in Table 1 match, but the pair in Table 2 does not. In this paper, we explore possibilities for matching these annotations based on set similarity functions of the syntactic heads of the spans.

[1]https://iptc.org/standards/media-topics/

4 Matching annotations

In this section, we describe the methods we used to evaluate different annotation matching functions. We call a *matching function* a function that takes two annotations as input. It returns True if they match and False if they do not.

4.1 Extracting the syntactic heads of annotations

We described a need for matching functions that emulate human judgment. Intuitively, we consider annotations to match if the "semantic core" of their constructions agree. Given a pair of annotations like [*There were several violations — There were several violations severe enough to talk about a breach of confidence*], we would roughly identify *"violations"* as the core element of the event described. If two annotations share the same semantic core, we consider them to match. Conversely, in the pair [*There were several violations severe enough to talk about a breach of confidence — a breach of confidence*], the semantic cores are different and the annotations do not match. The *"breach of confidence"* is not the focus of the first event mention.

We intuitively correlated the idea of semantic cores with the syntactic heads of the mention. In order to derive these syntactic heads, the state-of-the-art Alpino dependency parser for Dutch was used (van Noord, 2006). Using these parse trees, we extracted the set of *head tokens* from each annotation. We define a head token as any token that has "HD" as a dependency label in its node, or whose node is a child (directly or not) of a HD node. In an Alpino parse, the label HD is used to mark the verb in any verbal construction, the nominal core of a nominal construction, the preposition in a prepositional phrase and the core elements of adverbial groups (van Noord et al., 2018). Table 2 shows the syntactic heads extracted in this way from two non-matching annotations. Figure 2 shows a visualization of the syntactic tree obtained from the same example.[2]

[2]Visualized via `http://nederbooms.ccl.kuleuven.be/eng/alpinotree`.

Figure 1: Example of two fully annotated event mentions in the IAA corpus.
Translation: *Salah Abdeslam was questioned once again on Wednesday about his complicity in the attacks in Paris, which took place exactly two years and two days ago.*

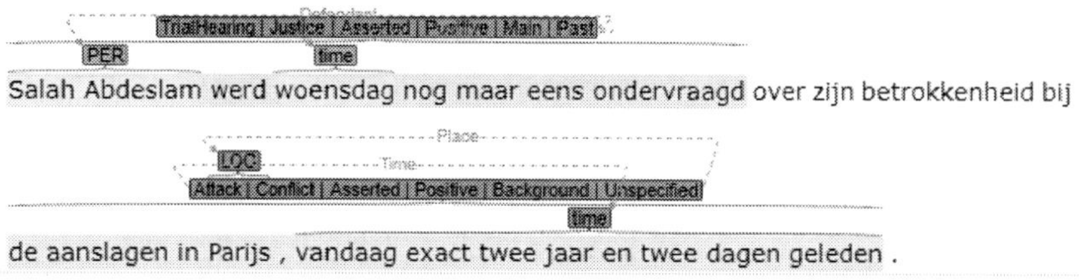

Annotator A	Annotator B
(1) Trump geeft VN kritiek bij eerste speech *Trump criticizes UN during first speech*	Trump geeft VN kritiek *Trump criticizes UN*
(2) Er waren herhaaldelijke inbreuken *There were several violations*	Er waren herhaaldelijke inbreuken die zwaar genoeg zijn om te spreken van een vertrouwensbreuk *There were several violations severe enough to talk about a breach of confidence*
(3) De Amerikaanse president Donald Trump heeft voor het eerst de Algemene Vergadering van de Verenigde Naties toegesproken. *The American president Donald Trump has addressed the General Assembly of the United Nations for the first time.*	De Amerikaanse president Donald Trump heeft voor het eerst de Algemene Vergadering van de Verenigde Naties toegesproken *The American president Donald Trump has addressed the General Assembly of the United Nations for the first time*

Table 1: Examples of matching overlapping mentions.

4.2 Match function candidates

The matching functions we explore in this paper score an annotation pair by the set similarity of their syntactic head sets. At the same time, a series of functions which use the set similarity of the token sets is also evaluated in order to test the relative advantage of using head over token sets, if any.

The similarity score is defined as the Dice coefficient between the two sets. This is the same measure used by Liu et al. (2015) to measure the similarity between event annotation token sets, and is equivalent to F1. The Dice coefficient returns a score between 0 and 1, where 1 equals complete overlap.

$$
\begin{aligned}
Dice(S_i, S_j) &= \frac{2|S_i S_j|}{|S_i| + |S_j|} \\
&= \frac{2}{|S_i|/|S_i S_j| + |S_j|/|S_i S_j|} \\
= F1(S_i, S_j) &= \frac{2}{1/P + 1/R}
\end{aligned}
$$

We set various thresholds over this score to achieve boolean functions. For instance, given an annotation pair (a_i, b_i) with a head set Dice coefficient of 0.6, a Dice-based matching function with a threshold of 0.5 will return True, and one with a threshold of 0.8 will return False. Finding a Dice-based function that emulates human behaviour means finding the right threshold at which the Dice function will maximally agree with the human evaluator. Note that at a threshold of 0, a Dice function will always return True, and at threshold 1 it will return False for anything less than exact overlap between the sets.

We designed and evaluated two baseline functions and two families of Dice-based functions, for a total of 40 matching functions:

- A random function that returns True or False with equal likelihood, which can be considered a baseline.
- A function which returns True if the tokens of both annotations match after punctuation has been removed.

Annotator A	Annotator B
De Amerikaanse president Donald Trump heeft voor het eerst de Algemene Vergadering van de Verenigde Naties toegesproken *The American president Donald Trump addressed the General Assembly of the United Nations for the first time*	de Algemene Vergadering van de Verenigde Naties *the General Assembly of the United Nations*
[president, heeft, vergadering, van, verenigde naties, toegesproken]	[vergadering, van, verenigde naties]

Table 2: Overlapping but non-matching mentions and the sets of their syntactic heads.

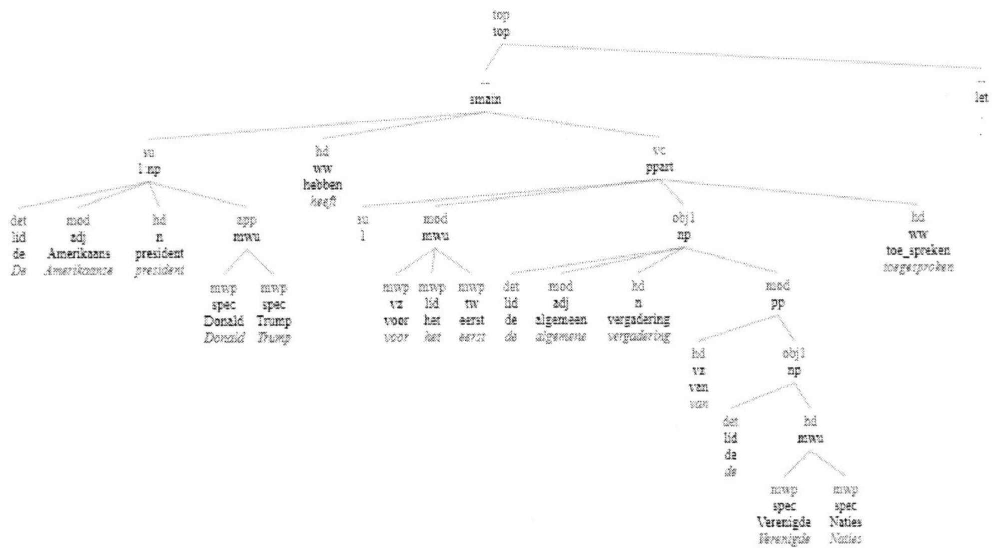

Figure 2: Visualization of an Alpino dependency tree used to extract syntactic heads.

- A series of 19 Dice-based threshold functions which run over the head sets of the annotation pair. Thresholds were chosen from the range $[0, 1]$ with a step of 0.05 (so the series of $[0.05, 0.1, 0.15, ..., 0.95, 1]$).
- The same series of 19 Dice functions operating over token sets.

4.3 The process of evaluating matching functions

To test the performance of a matching function, we compare its output to the judgment of a human evaluator. To this purpose, four additional news articles were selected and annotated by the same four annotators from the IAA set and judged by an independent human evaluator.[3] The goal of this evaluation is to discover how close the candidate fuzzy matching functions we designed come to matching the judgment of a human evaluator, and which of these candidates should be applied in the IAA study proper. In this section, we describe the actual evaluation process itself which consists of four phases.

(i) Collecting annotations Given two annotators, A and B, we attempt to match the annotations they made over a given sentence s. That is, for every pair of partial annotations over s, a human evaluator judges whether the pair matches or not; the fuzzy matching functions are run over the same pair and scored on how they agree with the human evaluator. Let a_i be A's annotations over s and b_i B's annotations over s. All pairs of annotations over a_i and b_i are collected: $[a_1b_1$, a_1b_2, a_1b_3, ...$]$. The Dice coefficient is symmetrical,

[3] As we will explain later, there is a negative skew in this dataset which must be taken into account.

such that the results over $(a_1 b_1)$ are equal to the results over $(b_1 a_1)$. Accordingly, only one of each such pairs is included.

(ii) Overlap filter A first filter function checks the overlap between the two annotated strings in each pair. If they overlap perfectly, the pair is counted as a matching pair without going through human evaluation or fuzzy matching. If they do not overlap at all, they are counted as not matching. At the end of the first filter, the annotation pairs are sorted in three sets: O_T, the set of perfectly overlapping annotations; O_P, the set of partially overlapping annotations, and O_F, the set of non-overlapping annotations.

(iii) Human and system evaluations Human and system evaluation is only performed on O_P. The human evaluator and each fuzzy matching function judge each pair as matching or not matching. We denote the set of pairs that the human evaluator judges as matching to H_T when they match and to H_F when they do not. For a given candidate matching function C, we obtain similar sets C_T and C_F.

(iv) Scoring The judgment of the human evaluator is taken as the gold standard answer. Each function is then scored based on its agreement with the human evaluation. For a candidate function C, we count the number of pairs on which it agrees with the human annotator as n_{Agr}. The score of a function is the ratio of the number of agreements over the total number of partially overlapping annotations.

$$n_{Agr} = |H_T \cap C_T| + |H_F \cap C_F|$$
$$S = \frac{n_{Agr}}{|O_P|}$$

It reads as a number between 0 and 1, where 1 represents total agreement with the human evaluator.

5 Results

In total, 182 annotation pairs were collected. Table 3 summarizes set statistics after phases (i) to (iii). Of the 182 pairs, 44 overlapped perfectly and 77 not at all. Of the remaining 61 partially overlapping pairs, the human annotator counted 44 pairings as false and 16 as true. The negative skew indicates that most overlapping annotations are not the same events annotated differently, but simply mentions of different events that happen to overlap (e.g. Table 2).

Set of pairs	Count
Total	182
O_T	44
O_P	61
O_F	77
H_T	17
H_F	44

Table 3: Annotation pair statistics over the four evaluation documents.

Matching function	Score
Random match (baseline)	0.43
Punctuation removed (baseline)	0.79
Dice 0.0 (head or token)	0.28
Dice 0.75, 0.8 (head)	**0.89**
Dice 1.0 (head)	0.79
Dice 0.75-0.90 (token)	0.85
Dice 1.0 (token)	0.72

Table 4: Results of the different matching functions

Table 4 reports on the different matching functions (Section 4.2). The reported random score is the average over three runs, and obtains a score of 0.43. This can be read as agreement with the human evaluator in 43% of cases. We single out a few results from the Dice functions. Dice 0.0 on heads or tokens always returns True and agrees in 28% of cases. Dice 1.0 on tokens always returns False by definition, since it expects perfect overlap of token sets but is only run on partially overlapping sets. It scores 0.72. The negative skew in the dataset is evident in these two results. Dice 1.0 on heads returns True only if the heads sets of the annotation pairs match exactly. It intuitively works well in cases where there is little diversity in annotated spans, and disagreements revolve around insignificant elements or punctuation marks. It scores 0.79. As a comparison, we tested a baseline which return True if the tokens of each annotation match exactly after punctuation has been discarded, which also scores 0.79.

Table 5 gives the scores for Dice functions on each threshold. The small size of the set prevents us from tuning the Dice threshold on a separate development set; we therefore present scores for all functions. The strictly best-performing function was found to be Dice on heads with thresholds 0.75 or 0.8, with a top score of 0.89, indicated in bold in Table 4. The Dice functions on tokens plateau between thresholds 0.75 to 0.90 with a score of 0.85. We therefore found head-based matching to outperform token-based matching by 4 percentage points.

Since this scoring method omits the judgments made in the overlap filter phase (phase (ii) in Section 4.3), we also calculated a *full score* which reflects the function's performance if the judgments of phase (ii) are taken into account as well

$$S_{Full} = \frac{n_{Agr} + |O_T| + |O_F|}{|O_P| + |O_T| + |O_F|}$$

With this measure, Dice 0.75-0.80 on heads scores 0.96, and Dice 0.75-0.90 on tokens scores 0.95. The relative advantage of using heads is less apparent in these measures, since partial matches constitute only 61 of 182 total annotation pairs. In other words, about two thirds of pairs are judged during phase (ii), such that the effect of fuzzy matching is less pronounced.

Dice threshold	On heads	On tokens
1.0	0.79	0.72
0.95	0.79	0.80
0.9	0.82	**0.85**
0.85	0.85	**0.85**
0.8	**0.89**	**0.85**
0.75	**0.89**	**0.85**
0.7	0.70	0.84
0.65	0.69	0.84
0.6	0.67	0.85
0.55	0.67	0.74
0.5	0.66	0.54
0.45	0.66	0.51
0.4	0.62	0.44
0.35	0.56	0.44
0.3	0.54	0.39
0.25	0.44	0.36
0.2	0.39	0.31
0.15	0.34	0.31
0.1	0.34	0.28
0.05	0.34	0.28
0.0	0.28	0.28

Table 5: Scores of all Dice functions.

6 Discussion and conclusion

This pilot study evaluated a set of 40 fuzzy matching functions to match event annotations over different annotators for use in consistency studies. In our corpus, annotations span several tokens by default, and there is a considerable gray zone where annotators may mark the same event but disagree on the exact span. To perform an inter-annotator study in this context, it is necessary to have fuzzy matching functions that can determine whether overlapping annotations match or refer to different events. An evaluation set of 182 potentially matching annotation pairs was devised and functions were tested against the judgment of a human evaluator.

Our intuition was that matching functions which leverage the syntactic heads of the annotation, presumed to be the "semantic centers" of the span, would outperform token-based fuzzy matching methods. Head-based functions were indeed found to perform best overall, with a score of 0.89 for the Dice 0.75-0.80 functions on heads. Therefore, we show that the fuzzy matching functions we devised emulate human judgment more closely than the baseline, and that functions using syntactic heads perform better than token-based functions. Given these results we will proceed with the best-performing head-based matching function for our corpus IAA study.

As future work we wish to conduct a more fine-grained exploration of the resulting dependency trees, which could further benefit matching by restricting the concept of syntactic heads. We took as heads the nodes tagged as "HD" in the dependency tree or the descendants of these nodes; these include the prepositions in prepositional phrases and the cores of adverbial groups. Filtering out these heads would further reduce the head sets of annotations to essential elements. Additionally, heads could be limited to nodes appearing in the top few levels of the tree. Conversely, relying more on parsing information implies a risk of error propagation, where errors made in parsing percolate into matching. We also wish to investigate which, if any, impact this has on the results.

Acknowledgements

We thank the reviewers for their helpful comments. This work was supported by #NewsDNA (Ghent University, Belgium), an interdisciplinary research project aimed at developing and testing an algorithm that uses news diversity as a key driver for personalised news recommendation. `http://newsdna.ugent.be`.

References

2008. *ACE English Annotation Guidelines for Events (v5.4.3)*. Linguistics Data Consortium.

Jacqueline Aguilar, Charley Beller, Paul McNamee, Benjamin Van Durme, Stephanie Strassel, Zhiyi Song, and Joe Ellis. 2014. A Comparison of the Events and Relations Across ACE , ERE , TAC-KBP , and FrameNet Annotation Standards.

Jun Araki and Teruko Mitamura. 2015. Joint Event Trigger Identification and Event Coreference Resolution with Structured Perceptron. In *Proceedings of the 2015 Conference on Empirical Methods in Natural Language Processing*, pages 2074–2080, Lisbon, Portugal. Association for Computational Linguistics.

Jun Araki and Teruko Mitamura. 2018. Open-Domain Event Detection using Distant Supervision. In *Proceedings of the 27th International Conference on Computational Linguistics*, pages 878–891, Santa Fe, New Mexico, USA. Association for Computational Linguistics.

Agata Cybulska and Piek Vossen. 2014. Using a sledgehammer to crack a nut? Lexical diversity and event coreference resolution. *Proceedings of the Ninth International Conference on Language Resources and Evaluation (LREC'14)*, pages 4545–4552.

George Doddington, Alexis Mitchell, Mark Przybocki, Lance Ramshaw, Stephanie Strassel, and Ralph Weischedel. 2004. The Automatic Content Extraction (ACE) Program Tasks, Data, and Evaluation. In *Proceedings of LREC*.

Ralph Grishman. 2010. The Impact of Task and Corpus on Event Extraction Systems. *Lrec*, pages 2928–2931.

Oana Inel and Lora Aroyo. 2019. Validation methodology for expert-annotated datasets: Event annotation case study. In *2nd Conference on Language, Data and Knowledge, LDK 2019*, page 12. Schloss Dagstuhl- Leibniz-Zentrum fur Informatik GmbH, Dagstuhl Publishing.

Qi Li, Heng Ji, Yu Hong, and Sujian Li. 2014. Constructing information networks using one single model. *Methods on Natural Language Processing (EMNLP2014)*, pages 1846–1851.

Qi Li, Heng Ji, and Liang Huang. 2013. Joint Event Extraction via Structured Prediction with Global Features. *Proceedings of the 51st Annual Meeting of the Association for Computational Linguistics (Volume 1: Long Papers)*, pages 73–82.

Zhengzhong Liu, Teruko Mitamura, and Eduard Hovy. 2015. Evaluation Algorithms for Event Nugget Detection : A Pilot Study. In *Proceedings of the The 3rd Workshop on EVENTS: Definition, Detection, Coreference, and Representation*, pages 53–57, Denver, Colorado. Association for Computational Linguistics.

Jing Lu and Vincent Ng. 2017. Joint Learning for Event Coreference Resolution. pages 90–101. Association for Computational Linguistics.

Jing Lu and Vincent Ng. 2018. Event Coreference Resolution: A Survey of Two Decades of Research. In *Proceedings of the Twenty-Seventh International Joint Conference on Artificial Intelligence*, pages 5479–5486, Stockholm, Sweden. International Joint Conferences on Artificial Intelligence Organization.

Anne-Lyse Minard, Manuela Speranza, Ruben Urizar, Marieke van Erp, Anneleen Schoen, and Chantal van Son. 2016. MEANTIME, the NewsReader Multilingual Event and Time Corpus. In *Proceedings of the 10th language resources and evaluation conference (LREC 2016)*, page 6, Portoro, Slovenia. European Language Resources Association (ELRA).

Teruko Mitamura, Yukari Yamakawa, Susan Holm, Zhiyi Song, Ann Bies, Seth Kulick, and Stephanie Strassel. 2015. Event Nugget Annotation: Processes and Issues. In *Proceedings of the The 3rd Workshop on EVENTS: Definition, Detection, Coreference, and Representation*, pages 66–76, Denver, Colorado. Association for Computational Linguistics.

National Institute of Standards and Technology. 2005. The ACE 2005 (ACE05) Evaluation Plan. Technical report.

G. J. van Noord. 2006. At Last Parsing Is Now Operational.

Gertjan van Noord, Ineke Schuurman, and Gosse Bouma. 2018. Lassy Syntactische Annotatie (Revision 19456). page 208.

Tim O'Gorman, Kristin Wright-Bettner, and Martha Palmer. 2016. Richer Event Description: Integrating event coreference with temporal, causal and bridging annotation. *Proceedings of the 2nd Workshop on Computing News Storylines (CNS 2016)*, pages 47–56.

Haoruo Peng, Kai-Wei Chang, and Dan Roth. 2015. A Joint Framework for Coreference Resolution and Mention Head Detection. In *Proceedings of the Nineteenth Conference on Computational Natural Language Learning*, pages 12–21, Beijing, China. Association for Computational Linguistics.

Haoruo Peng, Yangqi Song, and Dan Roth. 2016. Event Detection and Co-reference with Minimal Supervision. *Emnlp*, pages 392–402.

Piek Vossen. 2016. *Newsreader public summary*, volume 31.

Piek Vossen, Filip Ilievski, Marten Postma, and Segers Roxane. 2018. Don't Annotate, but Validate: a Data-to-Text Method for Capturing Event Data. In *LREC2018, Myazaki*.

Seid Muhie Yimam, Chris Biemann, Richard Eckart de Castilho, and Iryna Gurevych. 2014. Automatic Annotation Suggestions and Custom Annotation Layers in WebAnno. In *Proceedings of 52nd Annual Meeting of the Association for Computational Linguistics: System Demonstrations*, pages 91–96, Baltimore, Maryland. Association for Computational Linguistics.

A Dataset of Crowdsourced Word Sequences: Collections and Answer Aggregation for Ground Truth Creation

Jiyi Li
University of Yamanashi, Kofu, Japan
RIKEN AIP, Tokyo, Japan
jyli@yamanashi.ac.jp

Fumiyo Fukumoto
University of Yamanashi, Kofu, Japan
fukumoto@yamanashi.ac.jp

Abstract

The target outputs of many NLP tasks are word sequences. To collect the data for training and evaluating models, the crowd is a cheaper and easier to access than the oracle. To ensure the quality of the crowdsourced data, people can assign multiple workers to one question and then aggregate the multiple answers with diverse quality into a golden one. How to aggregate multiple crowdsourced word sequences with diverse quality is a curious and challenging problem. People need a dataset for addressing this problem. We thus create a dataset (CrowdWSA2019) which contains the translated sentences generated from multiple workers. We provide three approaches as the baselines on the task of extractive word sequence aggregation. Specially, one of them is an original one we propose which models the reliability of workers. We also discuss some issues on ground truth creation of word sequences which can be addressed based on this dataset.

1 Introduction

For many tasks in NLP area, the target outputs are word sequences. To train and evaluate the models, the ground truth in the form of word sequences are required. Instead of the oracle which is expensive and has an insufficient number, the crowd which is cheaper and easier to access is a good alternative for collecting the gold standard data.

Because the ability of crowd workers is diverse, to guarantee the quality of the collected data, one solution is to generate redundant data by assigning multiple workers to one instance and then aggregate the multiple answers into golden ones. How to aggregate multiple word sequences with diverse quality is a research problem. In NLP areas such as machine translation, although a few evaluation metrics (Liu et al., 2016) such as BLEU (Papineni et al., 2002) can use multiple golden answers for an instance, because the multiple crowdsourced answers are not golden ones, the aggregation approach for generating a golden one based on these crowdsourced answers is indispensable.

In crowdsourcing area, there are many existing work on answer aggregation for labels (Dawid and Skene, 1979; Whitehill et al., 2009; Zheng et al., 2017). Snow et al. (2008) evaluated crowdsourced label annotations for some NLP tasks and used majority voting for label aggregation. However, there is little work on answer aggregation for word sequences. Nguyen et al. (2017) proposed an aggregation method based on HMM for a sequence of categorical labels and needs to be improved for aligning sparse and free word sequences. If treating a word as a category, there are tens of thousands categories and a sequence only contains a small number of them. To address the problem of answer aggregation for word sequences, people need the datasets which contain multiple word sequence answers provided by different crowd workers for one instance. However, we find that most of the existing datasets in NLP area only contain a single golden answer for one instance.

In this paper, we create a dataset with several crowdsourced word sequence collections for the purpose of solving this problem through a real-world crowdsourcing platform. It contains the translated sentences of the target language by multiple workers from the sentences of the source language. The source sentences are extracted from several existing machine translation datasets. The raw target sentences in these existing datasets can be utilized for evaluating the quality of the crowdsourced data and the performance of the answer aggregation approaches. Our exploration study gives an analysis of worker quality in this dataset.

We provide several approaches on this dataset for the task of extractive sequence aggregation on crowdsourced word sequences, which extracts the

Proceedings of the First Workshop on Aggregating and Analysing Crowdsourced Annotations for NLP, pages 24–28
Hong Kong, China, November 3, 2019. ©2019 Association for Computational Linguistics
https://doi.org/10.18653/v1/P17

good word sequence from the candidates. One of them is our original approach which models the reliability of workers, because worker reliability is regarded as an important factor in label aggregation approaches (Zheng et al., 2017).

2 Datasets

2.1 Data Collections: CrowdWSA2019

A number of NLP tasks have the target outputs in the form of word sequences, e.g., machine translation, text summarization, question and answering and so on. In different tasks, the properties of the word sequences, e.g., text length and syntax, can be different from each other. In this paper, without loss of generality, we create a dataset[1] based on the machine translation task which uses short and complete sentences.

To collect the crowdsourced data, we first chose some collections of raw sentence pairs from the existing bilingual parallel corpora. The corpora we utilized are Japanese-English parallel corpora, i.e., JEC Basic Sentence Data[2] (one collection extracted, named as J1) and Tanaka Corpus[3] (two collections extracted, named as T1 and T2). We utilized Japanese as the source language and English as the target language.

We uploaded the sentences in the source language (denoted as *question*) to a real world crowdsourcing platform[4]. We asked the crowd workers to provide the translations in the target language (named as *answer*). Each crowdsourcing micro-task contained ten random source sentences in random order. A worker completed the sentences in a micro-task each time and can answer several random micro-tasks. For the evaluation based on this dataset, we can utilize the original sentences in the target language (named as *true answer*) of these raw sentence pairs to compare with the crowdsourced data and the aggregated word sequences (named as *estimated true answer*).

For the quality of the collected data, because the purpose of creating this dataset is to verify the word sequence aggregation methods, it would be better if the answers of word sequences have diverse quality. The crowd workers on the crowdsourcing platform are mainly Japanese native speakers and non-native speakers of English. Their English abilities are diverse. In the task description, we also encouraged the English beginners to join and provide answers so that the collected answers have diverse quality. Note that if the purpose is collecting high-quality annotation data for specific NLP tasks such as machine translation, using experts or native speakers would be better for improving the data quality.

data	#que.	#wor.	#ans.	#apq	mmr
J1	250	70	2,490	9.96	0.1423
T1	100	42	1,000	10	0.5929
T2	100	43	1,000	10	0.5791

Table 1: Number of questions, workers and answers. #apq: average number of Answers Per Question. mmr: worker-question answer Matrix Missing Rate.

2.2 Exploration Study

We explore some properties of these collections. First, Table 1 lists the statistics of the three collections. Besides the number of questions, workers and answers, it also shows two measures. $\#apq$ is the average number of Answers Per Question. It shows the redundancy of the answers. mmr is the worker-question answer Matrix Missing Rate. It shows the sparsity of the answers. Our collections follows the practical scenario, i.e., when the number of questions is huge, it is impossible that each worker can answer all questions. The redundancy and sparsity may influence the results of answer aggregation approach. For example, it has been shown that the performance of some aggregation approaches for categorical labels may degrade when the mmr is low (Li et al., 2017).

Second, we show the answer quality in the data. Figure 1 illustrates the distribution of answer reliability by embedding similarity. We measure the similarity between a worker answer and the true answer of a question to evaluate the quality. We use the universal sentence encoder to encode the sentences (Cer et al., 2018) into embeddings, and compute the cosine similarity between the embeddings of two sentences. The reliability of a worker is the mean similarity for all answers of this worker. This reliability of a question is the mean similarity of all answers of this question. Both the mean of two types of reliability are in the range of [0.7, 0.8]. The quality on both T1 and T2 is higher. One possible reason is that the size

[1] https://github.com/garfieldpigljy/CrowdWSA2019

[2] http://nlp.ist.i.kyoto-u.ac.jp/EN/index.php?JEC%20Basic%20Sentence%20Data

[3] https://github.com/odashi/small_parallel_enja

[4] https://www.lancers.jp/

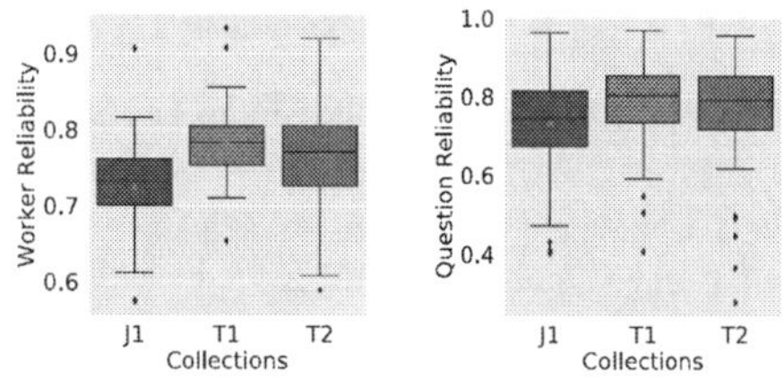

(a) Worker-Wise (b) Question-Wise

Figure 1: Answer Reliability by Embedding Similarity

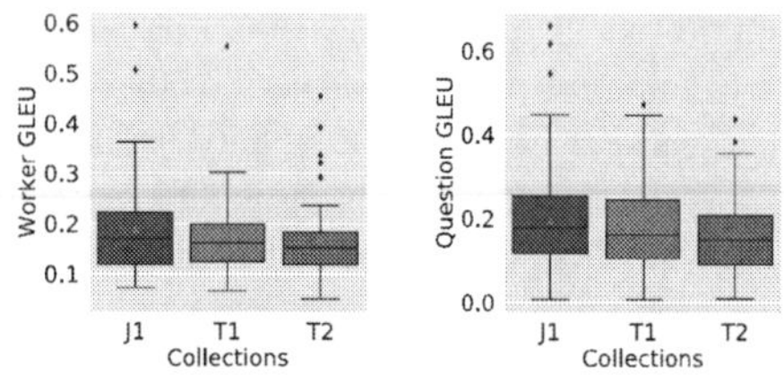

(a) Worker-Wise (b) Question-Wise

Figure 2: Answer Reliability by GLEU

of J1 is larger and more low quality workers join the task, while the high quality workers on a non-native English crowdsourcing platform is limited.

Figure 2 shows the distribution of answer reliability measured by GLEU (Wu et al., 2016). To be consistent with the reliability of workers and questions computed by embedding similarity, we use the mean of sentence-wise GLEU of all answers of a worker (question), in contrast to corpus-wise BLEU measure. In contrast to Figure 1, the quality on J1 is higher. One possible reason is that the low quality workers judged by embedding similarity can provide good words or phrases translations which the GLEU focuses on, but cannot provide good word orders and syntax on the sentence level which the DAN (Iyyer et al., 2015) model of universal sentence encoder considers.

3 Extractive Answer Aggregation

When we obtain multiple answers for a given question, we need to aggregate them into one answer which can be used as the golden data in the collected dataset. There are at least two alternatives of answer aggregation approaches for the case of word sequence, i.e., extractive and abstractive answer aggregation. Extractive aggregation methods extract the potential optimal one from multiple worker answers; abstractive aggregation methods generate a new answer by analyzing and understanding all of the worker answers. In the research area of crowdsourcing, most of the existing work of answer aggregation focus on categorical or numerical labels (Zheng et al., 2017). They estimate a pre-defined category or value and thus are extractive approaches. In this paper, we focus on the baselines of extractive answer aggregation.

We define question set $\mathcal{Q} = \{q_i\}_i$, worker set $\mathcal{W} = \{w_k\}_k$, answer set $\mathcal{A} = \{a_i^k\}_{i,k}$, true answer set $\mathcal{Z} = \{z_i\}_i$ and estimated true answer set $\hat{\mathcal{Z}} = \{\hat{z}_i\}_i$. The answer set of a question is $\mathcal{L}_i$; the answer set of a worker is $\mathcal{V}_k$. The encoder is $e(\cdot)$. We use cosine similarity for sim computation.

3.1 Sequence Majority Voting

Majority voting is one of the most typical answer aggregation approaches. For the specific data type of word sequences, we adapt it into a Sequence Majority Voting (SMV) approach. For each question, it first estimates the embeddings of the true answers by $\hat{e}_i = mean(e(\mathcal{L}_i))$; after that it extracts the worker answer $\hat{z}_i = \arg\max_{a_i^k} sim(e(a_i^k), \hat{e}_i)$ as the true answer.

3.2 Sequence Maximum Similarity

We adapt the method in Kobayashi (2018), which is proposed as a post-ensemble method for multiple summarization generation models. For each question, it extracts the worker answer which has largest sum of similarity with other answers of this question. It can be regarded as creating a kernel density estimator and extract the maximum density answer. The kernel function uses the cosine similarity. This Sequence Maximum Similarity (SMS) method can be formulated as $\hat{z}_i = \arg\max_{a_i^{k_1}} \sum_{k_1 \neq k_2} sim(e(a_i^{k_1}), e(a_i^{k_2}))$.

3.3 Reliability Aware Sequence Aggregation

Both SMV and SMS do not consider the worker reliability. In crowdsourcing, worker reliability is diverse and is a useful information for estimating true answers. Existing work in the categorical answer aggregation strengthen the influences of answers provided by the workers with higher reliability. Therefore, we also propose an approach which models the worker reliability, named as Reliability Aware Sequence Aggregation (RASA).

The RASA approach is as follows. (1). ENCODER: it encodes the worker answers into embeddings; (2). ESTIMATION: it estimates the embeddings of the true answers considering worker reliability; (3). EXTRACTION: for each question, it extracts a worker answer which is most similar with the embeddings of the estimated true answer.

For estimating the embeddings of the true answers, we adapt the CATD approach (Li et al., 2014) which is proposed for aggregating multiple numerical ratings. We extend it into our sequence case by adapting it to the sequence embeddings. We define the worker reliability as β. The method iteratively estimates β_k and $\hat{e}_i$ until convergence, $\beta_k = \frac{\chi^2_{(\alpha/2,|\mathcal{V}_k|)}}{\sum(e(a_i^k)-\hat{e}_i)^2}$, $\hat{e}_i = \frac{\sum \beta_k e(a_i^k)}{\sum \beta_k}$, where χ^2 is the chi-squared distribution and the significance level α is set as 0.05 empirically. We initialize $\hat{e}_i$ by using the SMV approach. SMS does not estimate $\hat{e}_i$ and cannot initialize $\hat{e}_i$.

3.4 Experimental Results

The evaluation metric is GLEU and the average similarity between the embeddings of the estimated true answers and the true answers (the original target sentences in the corpus) on the all questions. For the extractive answer aggregation, there exists theoretical optimal performance. It is the performance of selecting the worker answer with largest embedding similarity (or GLEU) with the true answer. Table 2 lists the results.

data	SMV	SMS	RASA	Optimal
J1	0.7354	**0.7969**	0.7914	0.8853
T1	0.7851	0.8377	**0.8451**	0.9047
T2	0.7696	0.8288	**0.8339**	0.8986

(a) Embedding Similarity

data	SMV	SMS	RASA	Optimal
J1	0.1930	**0.2627**	0.2519	0.4990
T1	0.1740	0.2194	**0.2296**	0.3698
T2	0.1616	0.2170	**0.2345**	0.3637

(b) GLEU

Table 2: Results of extractive answer aggregation. The optimal result is the theoretical optimal performance of the collection for extractive answer aggregation.

First, both SMS and RASA outperform the naïve baseline SMV. RASA is better than SMV because it considers the worker reliability. SMS is better than SMV as it is based on kernel density estimation which is more sophisticated than majority voting. Second, SMS performs best on J1 collection and RASA performs better on T1 and T2 collection. One of the possible reasons is that J1 has more low quality workers. RASA tends to strengthen the influences of major workers. The estimated embeddings are near to the answers of "good" workers and the "good" workers are the ones that the embeddings of their answers are near to the estimated embeddings. If there are many low-quality workers, it is possible to mistakenly regard a low-quality worker as a high-quality worker because this worker may provide more similar answers with other (low-quality) workers. RASA thus may strengthen the answer by a low-quality worker. Third, the results on both embedding similarity and GLEU are consistent. Forth, in the theoretical optimal results, the quality of J1 is higher than T1 and T2 on GLUE but lower on embedding similarity. This observation is consistent with that in Figure 1 and 2 in Section 2.2. Finally, all methods still cannot be close to the theoretical optimum. The performance is still possible to be improved.

4 Conclusion

In this paper, we proposed a dataset for the research of crowdsourced word sequence aggregation. We also provided three approaches on these datasets for the task of extractive aggregation for crowdsourced word sequences. One of them considers the worker reliability. There are some future work on this topic of answer aggregation.

First, for abstractive answer aggregation approach, an option is that we can train an encoder-decoder model to decode the estimated embeddings of the true answer into a word sequence which can be different from worker answers. Therefore, the abstractive approaches are possible to reach better results than the optimal results of the extractive approaches shown in Table 2.

Second, we can collect additional pairwise comparisons on the preferences of the worker answers by using another round of crowdsourcing tasks and extract the preferred answers. It is similar to a creator-evaluator framework (Baba and Kashima, 2013). Otani et al. (2016) proposed an approach for aggregating the results of multiple machine translation systems with pairwise comparisons. The typical approach of aggregating the pairwise comparison into a rank list was Bradley-Terry model (Bradley and Terry, 1952); CrowdBT model (Chen et al., 2013) extended it in crowdsourcing settings; Zhang et al. (2016) summarized more existing work.

Acknowledgments

This work was partially supported By JSPS KAKENHI Grant Number 17K00299 and 19K20277.

References

Yukino Baba and Hisashi Kashima. 2013. Statistical quality estimation for general crowdsourcing tasks. In *Proceedings of the 19th ACM SIGKDD International Conference on Knowledge Discovery and Data Mining*, KDD '13, pages 554–562, New York, NY, USA. ACM.

Ralph Allan Bradley and Milton E. Terry. 1952. Rank analysis of incomplete block designs: I. the method of paired comparisons. *Biometrika*, 39(3/4):324–345.

Daniel Cer, Yinfei Yang, Sheng-yi Kong, Nan Hua, Nicole Limtiaco, Rhomni St. John, Noah Constant, Mario Guajardo-Cespedes, Steve Yuan, Chris Tar, Yun-Hsuan Sung, Brian Strope, and Ray Kurzweil. 2018. Universal sentence encoder. *CoRR*, abs/1803.11175.

Xi Chen, Paul N. Bennett, Kevyn Collins-Thompson, and Eric Horvitz. 2013. Pairwise ranking aggregation in a crowdsourced setting. In *Proceedings of the Sixth ACM International Conference on Web Search and Data Mining*, WSDM '13, pages 193–202, New York, NY, USA. ACM.

A. P. Dawid and A. M. Skene. 1979. Maximum likelihood estimation of observer error-rates using the em algorithm. *Journal of the Royal Statistical Society. Series C (Applied Statistics)*, 28(1):20–28.

Mohit Iyyer, Varun Manjunatha, Jordan Boyd-Graber, and Hal Daumé III. 2015. Deep unordered composition rivals syntactic methods for text classification. In *Proceedings of the 53rd Annual Meeting of the Association for Computational Linguistics and the 7th International Joint Conference on Natural Language Processing (Volume 1: Long Papers)*, pages 1681–1691, Beijing, China. Association for Computational Linguistics.

Hayato Kobayashi. 2018. Frustratingly easy model ensemble for abstractive summarization. In *Proceedings of the 2018 Conference on Empirical Methods in Natural Language Processing*, pages 4165–4176, Brussels, Belgium. Association for Computational Linguistics.

Jiyi Li, Yukino Baba, and Hisashi Kashima. 2017. Hyper questions: Unsupervised targeting of a few experts in crowdsourcing. In *Proceedings of the 2017 ACM on Conference on Information and Knowledge Management*, CIKM '17, pages 1069–1078, New York, NY, USA. ACM.

Qi Li, Yaliang Li, Jing Gao, Lu Su, Bo Zhao, Murat Demirbas, Wei Fan, and Jiawei Han. 2014. A confidence-aware approach for truth discovery on long-tail data. *Proc. VLDB Endow.*, 8(4):425–436.

Chia-Wei Liu, Ryan Lowe, Iulian Serban, Mike Noseworthy, Laurent Charlin, and Joelle Pineau. 2016. How NOT to evaluate your dialogue system: An empirical study of unsupervised evaluation metrics for dialogue response generation. In *Proceedings of the 2016 Conference on Empirical Methods in Natural Language Processing*, pages 2122–2132, Austin, Texas. Association for Computational Linguistics.

An Thanh Nguyen, Byron Wallace, Junyi Jessy Li, Ani Nenkova, and Matthew Lease. 2017. Aggregating and predicting sequence labels from crowd annotations. In *Proceedings of the 55th Annual Meeting of the Association for Computational Linguistics (Volume 1: Long Papers)*, pages 299–309, Vancouver, Canada. Association for Computational Linguistics.

Naoki Otani, Toshiaki Nakazawa, Daisuke Kawahara, and Sadao Kurohashi. 2016. IRT-based aggregation model of crowdsourced pairwise comparison for evaluating machine translations. In *Proceedings of the 2016 Conference on Empirical Methods in Natural Language Processing*, pages 511–520, Austin, Texas. Association for Computational Linguistics.

Kishore Papineni, Salim Roukos, Todd Ward, and Wei-Jing Zhu. 2002. Bleu: A method for automatic evaluation of machine translation. In *Proceedings of the 40th Annual Meeting on Association for Computational Linguistics*, ACL '02, pages 311–318, Stroudsburg, PA, USA. Association for Computational Linguistics.

Rion Snow, Brendan O'Connor, Daniel Jurafsky, and Andrew Y. Ng. 2008. Cheap and fast—but is it good?: Evaluating non-expert annotations for natural language tasks. In *Proceedings of the Conference on Empirical Methods in Natural Language Processing*, EMNLP '08, pages 254–263, Stroudsburg, PA, USA. Association for Computational Linguistics.

Jacob Whitehill, Paul Ruvolo, Tingfan Wu, Jacob Bergsma, and Javier Movellan. 2009. Whose vote should count more: Optimal integration of labels from labelers of unknown expertise. In *Proceedings of the 22Nd International Conference on Neural Information Processing Systems*, NIPS'09, pages 2035–2043, USA. Curran Associates Inc.

Yonghui Wu, Mike Schuster, Zhifeng Chen, Quoc V Le, Mohammad Norouzi, Wolfgang Macherey, Maxim Krikun, Yuan Cao, Qin Gao, Klaus Macherey, et al. 2016. Google's neural machine translation system: Bridging the gap between human and machine translation. *arXiv preprint arXiv:1609.08144*.

Xiaohang Zhang, Guoliang Li, and Jianhua Feng. 2016. Crowdsourced top-k algorithms: An experimental evaluation. *Proc. VLDB Endow.*, 9(8):612–623.

Yudian Zheng, Guoliang Li, Yuanbing Li, Caihua Shan, and Reynold Cheng. 2017. Truth inference in crowdsourcing: Is the problem solved? *Proc. VLDB Endow.*, 10(5):541–552.

Crowd-sourcing annotation of complex NLU tasks: A case study of argumentative content annotation

Tamar Lavee, Lili Kotlerman*, Matan Orbach, Yonatan Bilu, Michal Jacovi, Ranit Aharonov and Noam Slonim
IBM Research

Abstract

Recent advancements in machine reading and listening comprehension involve the annotation of long texts. Such tasks are typically time consuming, making crowd-annotations an attractive solution, yet their complexity often makes such a solution unfeasible. In particular, a major concern is that crowd annotators may be tempted to skim through long texts, and answer questions without reading thoroughly. We present a case study of adapting this type of task to the crowd. The task is to identify claims in a several minute long debate speech. We show that sentence-by-sentence annotation does not scale and that labeling only a subset of sentences is insufficient. Instead, we propose a scheme for effectively performing the full, complex task with crowd annotators, allowing the collection of large scale annotated datasets. We believe that the encountered challenges and pitfalls, as well as lessons learned, are relevant in general when collecting data for large scale natural language understanding (NLU) tasks.

1 Introduction

The availability and scale of crowdsourcing platforms today has enabled the collection of large scale labeled datasets (Negri et al., 2011; Sabou et al., 2014; Rajpurkar et al., 2016, 2018; Choi et al., 2018). These datasets facilitate the use of advanced machine learning methods, which leverage such vast volumes of labeled data to achieve state-of-the-art performance on various tasks. Crowd annotation tasks are typically simple, short, and easy to explain, making them well-suited to the typically untrained temporary workforce. Some examples include named entity recognition (Finin et al., 2010), textual entailment (Mehdad et al., 2010) or generating facts from text (Wang and Callison-Burch, 2010). Complex tasks are typically broken into smaller, simpler chunks to suit these requirements (Wang et al., 2013). For example, Zeichner et al. (2012) break up their evaluation of inference rules into three simpler sub-tasks, and Scholman and Demberg (2017) simplify their discourse relation annotation task by casting it as a selection of a connecting phrase from a predefined list. Indeed, GLUE (Wang et al., 2018), a popular benchmark for NLU tasks, focuses only on annotations of single sentences or pairs of sentences, which tend to be simpler than those required in longer texts. However, task decomposition is not always feasible. As we discuss below, while a relevant decomposition scheme can be defined for our task, it does not allow performing the task in an effective and comprehensive way.

We describe the adaptation of a complex labeling task to the crowd: identifying claims in spoken argumentative content (for an example, see Figure 1). This work extends our previous study, in which annotation was performed by experts (Mirkin et al., 2018).

Obtaining such labeled data facilitates the development of language understanding systems which listen to speeches and identify claims therein. This, in turn, can serve as the basic building block for generating arguments rebutting these claims, or summarizing an argumentative text into the main claims made therein. Indeed, this annotation was made in the context of Project Debater, a system that can hold a debate with humans[1], where rebuttal was based on Argument Mining (Lavee et al., 2019) and general-purpose claims (Orbach et al., 2019).

At first glance, simplifying such a task could seem straightforward. By segmenting speeches

*Current affiliation: Intuition Robotics

[1]Demonstrated at Think 2019; https://www.youtube.com/watch?v=m3u-lyttrVw

Proceedings of the First Workshop on Aggregating and Analysing Crowdsourced Annotations for NLP, pages 29–38
Hong Kong, China, November 3, 2019.
https://doi.org/10.18653/v1/P17

Topic: We should end water fluoridation

Argumentative speech: We should continue fluoridating public water. Three arguments for this. The first is about why putting fluoride in the water is a public good. So recognize that tooth decay is a very serious problem in almost every country in the world because there's nothing that can be done to remedy it. People have one set of teeth for their adult life and unfortunately the high sugar, high acidity diets that most of us consume in today's world are pretty bad for your teeth. So it's essential that something is done to ensure that people don't have dental problems later in life. Water fluoridation is so cheap it's almost free. There are no proven side effects, despite billions of dollars spent in europe and america researching this, so I'm just going to throw out what will said earlier about the fact that some papers exist means this is unlikely to be safe. The FDA and comparable groups in europe have done lots and lots of tests and found that water fluoridation is actually a net health good, that there's no real risk to it. So we think that ultimately this is safe and that it has clear proven benefits to preserving your teeth later in life. At that point in the same way that we're okay with putting up guardrails on highways even though they might have some marginal cost, because they clearly save people's lives we do this thing. Look, maybe water fluoridation doesn't save anyone's life, but it obviously improves their quality of life in the long term. Not everyone can afford to have a dentist fluoridate their teeth, not everyone is going to be able to purchase these packets, but everyone drinks the tap water so we think that ultimately it's important that everyone has access to fluoride in order to preserve their own teeth for later in life. Our second argument is about why we think that it's okay for the government to paternalize and to put fluoride into the water. Two reasons. The first is that there's a compelling state interest. In most countries, although not my own, the government pays for people's dental health. So in places like britain maybe you have a co pay but ultimately if you're low income or going through a difficult time in terms of your job, the state will help you to pay for dentistry. What that means is that there's a clear state interest in minimizing the cost of people's visits to the dentist. Because fluoridation reduces the rate of cavities which are going to be the most expensive thing to have people get taken care of at the dentist, we tell you that ultimately there's a compelling state interest to put fluoride in the water. A couple of cents up front can save thousands of dollars later on root canals and other dental surgeries. We think that this compelling state interest is enough of a reason to paternalize. Especially because money for health is fungible. Any money that's spent on giving, you know, somebody who has a cavity a new set of teeth, could have been spent on helping a child with some sort of congenital illness. Ultimately we think it's important that we use our money as effectively as possible, that the state is frugal, and fluoridation is certainly that. And the second reason we think you can paternalize is because of the third party harms of not doing so. It may be true that adults can make a choice about whether or not to put fluoride in their water, but children really can't. They can only drink the water that they're given. At that point we think that children who can't choose to consent into this would be doing a lot of damage to their teeth and not rectifying it by using fluoride and ultimately they would suffer in the long term. We think the state needs to intervene to protect them. The third reason we think that we should put fluoride in the water is that it's not an undue burden on anyone. Will tries to tell you that it's unrealistic to ask people who don't want fluoride to drink bottled water. But I think it's an undue burden to ask everybody who wants healthy teeth to go out and buy fluoride so that a couple of hippies don't have to have fluoride in their water. This cuts both ways. We think that at the end of the day, bottled water, in the US at least, is so cheap it's almost free if you buy it in bulk. At that point we don't think it's an undue burden that the tiny minority of people who don't want fluoride have to spend a few dollars every week on water. So at the end of the day we think it's clear that the state should continue to fluoridate water. Thank you.

Potential claims:

1. Fluoridation is effective
2. Fluoridation is a great health achievement
3. Water fluoridation is critical for children
4. Fluoridation is safe
5. Water fluoridation is safe and important to dental health
6. Fluoridation of water is extremely beneficial for citizens, especially children
7. Fluoridation was a worthy project to improve the health
8. Water fluoridation is a safe and effective public health measure
9. Fluoridated water is safe
10. Water fluoridation is effective
11. Water fluoridation is safe, effective

Figure 1: A full example of the annotation task. Given a controversial topic, an argumentative speech discussing it, and a list of potential claims (relevant to the topic and of the same stance as the speech), the goal is determining which claims are mentioned in the speech. To appreciate the difficulty of the task, readers are encouraged to try to annotate this example themselves. The task is described in more detail in §2.

into sentences, it is possible to present a single sentence and a single claim, and ask whether the claim is made or mentioned in the sentence. However, this *sentence-level* setup has three major problems. First, there is a large number of sentence-claim pairs, which makes comprehensive labeling of all pairs unfeasible, even with crowdsourcing. For example, among the 200 speeches of Mirkin et al. (2018) a typical speech contains about 30 sentences, and is labeled vs. 4 claims. Thus, labeling the entire dataset requires labeling some 24,000 pairs. Second, the goal of the annotation process is to provide a fairly comprehensive sample of claims mentioned in speeches (e.g. for training a classifier), yet such pairs are rare. Thus, collecting a sizable amount of such pairs requires labeling a large amount of data. Third, labeling single sentences obscures their context, which may, in some cases, change how they are understood by annotators, thus affecting the collected labels. For example, a claim may not be explicit in a single sentence, but rather implied by a section of the speech.

An alternative to this approach is *speech-level* labeling – presenting an entire speech along with the full list of potential claims. This makes comprehensive labeling of entire speeches feasible, at the cost of added time and complexity. Annotation of a single speech takes at least several minutes of reading and/or listening, and long lists of claims often require iterating over the speech multiple times, since it is hard to memorize its full content in a single pass. It is tempting for an annotator who is not skilled at such tasks to only glimpse through the long text, rather than read it carefully. Conversely, a small, skilled workforce may be able to deal with a task of this complexity, but large-scale data collection by such a workforce is impractical.

To overcome these challenges, we suggest combining the advantages of both setups. Namely, comprehensive labeling of entire speeches using crowdsourcing. The main issue is to identify and motivate a reliable, skilled crowd workforce which is of sufficient size to perform it on a large scale. Similar works attempted to identify reliable crowd annotators based on their previous work (Ho et al., 2013), or other user characteristics like age or education (Li et al., 2014). Behavioral patterns during the task like scrolling and context switching have also been used to predict user reliability in crowdsourcing platforms (Goyal et al., 2018). Here, we rely on their suitability to our specific task, which requires unique skills like reading and listening comprehension and attention to nuance. During the annotation process, we monitor several features of each annotator (see §4), such as agreement with peers and labeling time, and use them to evaluate our confidence in their work. Based on these confidence measures, annotators determined as unreliable are filtered out, and strong ones are retained and rewarded. This monitoring also allowed to identify problems in our task design, which helped in adjusting it to the crowd.

Lastly, annotations from the two annotation schemes are compared, using pairs of claim and speech that were labeled in both (see §5).

The main contributions of this paper are: (i) Presenting a case study of long texts annotation in a complex NLU task, using crowdsourcing; (ii) A detailed description of a mechanism to select annotators that are reliable and qualified to the task using quality control measures taken from their work on our specific data; (iii) An analysis comparing an annotation setup which provides full textual context, to a simpler setup which obscures context information from annotators.

2 The annotation task

Listening comprehension over argumentative content is a new NLU task we recently introduced in Mirkin et al. (2018). This work included a corresponding dataset, annotated by experienced experts. Following is a description of that annotation task, which we now aim to adapt to the crowd.

Each annotation unit is presented in the context of a given controversial topic, such as *we should end water fluoridation*. It is comprised of two parts (see Figure 1): The first is a several-minute long speech, in which a single speaker is arguing for or against the given topic. The speeches are provided in both audio and text, allowing annotators a choice between listening, reading or both. The second part is a list of claims, potentially relevant to the topic and of the same stance as that of the speaker. The objective is identifying the subset of claims mentioned in a given speech. The resulting annotation is a set of speech–claim pairs, in which a pair is considered a *positive* match if the claim is mentioned in the speech (otherwise the pair is considered a *negative* match).

Specifically, annotators were instructed to consider a claim as mentioned in a speech if the statement *"The speaker argued that <claim>"* is true. This statement can be valid even if the speaker was stating the claim using a different phrasing or even if she did not explicitly express the claim, but merely implied it (see Example 1).

The full annotation guidelines are given in the Supplementary Materials.

Example 1 (Claim implied from a speech)

Claim: *Needle exchange reduces the spread of diseases*

Speech: *[...] Without the needle exchange program people are still going to do heroin or other kinds of drugs anyway with dirty or less safe needles. This does lead to things like HIV getting transmitted, it leads to other diseases as well, being more likely to get transmitted [...]*

---

3 Sentence-level annotation

In a *sentence-level* annotation scheme, the speech text is first split into sentences[2]. Then, pairs of sentence and claim are presented to annotators, who answer whether the claim is stated in the sentence. Figure 2 shows a screenshot of one annotation unit in this scheme. The questions are short, which is advantageous for crowdsourcing, and the collected answers indicate, in addition to whether a claim was mentioned in a speech, *where* was it mentioned, which is potentially important information for methods aimed at automatically identifying claims in speeches.

However, this scheme has three major limitations:

– ***Scalability***: Comprehensive labeling of all possible sentence-claim pairs is not feasible, even for crowdsourcing. A speech in our data contains, on average, 28.7 sentences, and has 65.6 claims which require annotation. This means having 1,882 claim and sentence pairs for each speech, and sums up to more than 2 million pairs for our data of 1,127 speeches.

A naive approach for reducing the number of pairs which require annotation is randomly sampling sentences from a given speech. However, because claims mentioned in speeches are typically mentioned only once or twice, such sampling would likely miss the mentioning sentences.

Another option is detecting sentences which are semantically similar to the claim, and annotating those with a high similarity. We tried doing so by using *word2vec* (Mikolov et al., 2013): a vector representation for a claim or a sentence was defined as the weighted-average of the vec-

[2]Using a manually created transcription of the audio into text, which includes sentence segmentation.

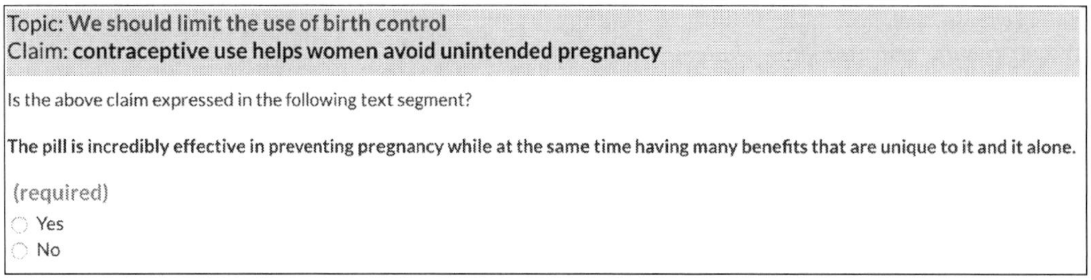

Figure 2: A screenshot of one unit within a *sentence-level* annotation scheme, including one claim-sentence pair.

tor representation of its words (using idf weights based on Wikipedia). The similarity between a claim and a sentence was then calculated using the cosine similarity between their vector representations. This increased the fraction of positive pairs, yet introduced a bias: pairs with definite lexical overlap were selected for labeling, but pairs where the claim is paraphrased or implicit were overlooked. Other selection options are possible, but they would likely introduce bias to the labeling process for similar reasons.

– *Limited context*: Deciding whether the claim is mentioned based on a single sentence can be difficult for two reasons. First, it is often hard to fully understand the speaker's intent when reading a single sentence. The sentence may refer to previous parts of the speech or contain an incomplete train of thought. Second, in many cases, a speaker clearly conveys a claim, yet it is not explicitly mentioned in any single sentence. Example 2 shows a claim expressed across several non-consecutive sentences.

Example 2 (Multi-sentence mentioned claim)
Claim: *Compulsory voting is undemocratic*
Speech: *Democracy is about protecting our rights [...] People have a right to not vote [...] We should respect literally any reason a person might not want to vote [...] We should ensure that that person is not penalized for not voting.*

– *Noisy negatives*: A claim mentioned in one of the speech sentences implies that it is mentioned in the speech, yet the opposite is not necessarily true. A prerequisite to establishing that a claim is *not* mentioned in a speech is its annotation as not mentioned *for every speech sentence*. Even then, it is possible that the claim arises from a combination of multiple sentences, and that when reviewing the entire speech, it would nonetheless be considered as mentioned. Thus, negative matches obtained in this scheme are a noisy approximation of the actual speech–claim negative examples.

4 Speech-level annotation

The above mentioned limitations of the sentence-level approach suggest that a different setup is desirable. We therefore considered a *speech-level* annotation scheme: annotators were provided with the full speech (text and audio) and a list of at most 20 claims from which they marked those mentioned (Speeches with more than 20 claims were shown more than once). Figure 3 illustrates one annotation unit in this scheme.

The main advantage of this approach is that the full context is available to annotators, making it easier to decide whether a certain idea was expressed. In addition, the collected negative matches are more reliable since annotators access the entire speech. However, this setup does not solve the scalability issue. Each unit is considerably more complex, since it requires the careful evaluation of a long text, while paying attention to nuances and subtleties. Thus, annotating a large volume of data in this scheme is even more challenging, since the common approach for scaling an annotation, namely the use of crowd, is typically applied to short, simple tasks.

Next, we experiment with this scheme using 3 different groups of annotators, using four measures: average pairwise kappa, fraction of high-agreement pairs, fraction of low-agreement pairs and fraction of positive pairs.

Average pairwise kappa is defined by first identifying annotators having at least 5 peers from their group with more than 20 common answers, and averaging their Cohen's Kappa score (Cohen, 1960) with each peer meeting these criteria. Then, the average over annotators is taken as the measure for the group. We note that the applicability of agreement measures like Cohen's Kappa to the crowd has been questioned, in particular for tasks

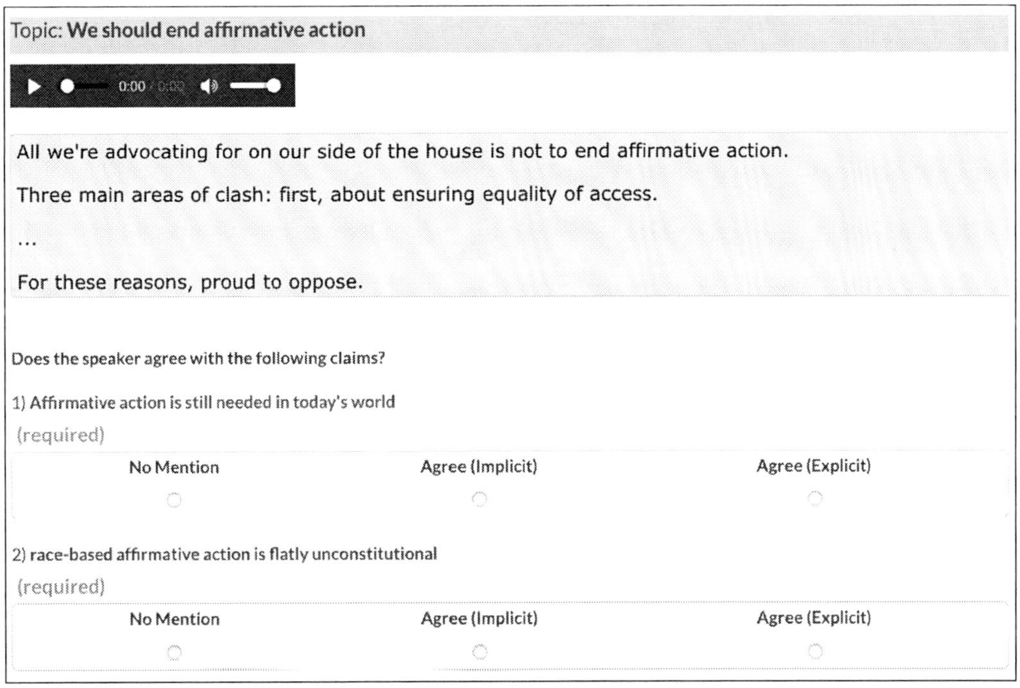

Figure 3: A screenshot of one unit within a *speech-level* annotation scheme. The unit contains a full speech (the full text is not shown due to space constraints) and a list of claims (partially shown).

within the argumentation domain (Passonneau and Carpenter, 2014; Habernal and Gurevych, 2016). Yet, while their exact value may be of limited interest, using them comparatively allows us to assess the reliability of results from different settings.

High-agreement and *Low-agreement* speech–claim pairs are defined by first defining the label of a pair as the majority vote of the annotators. If this majority includes at least 80% the of annotators, the pair is a *High agreement* pair. If it includes at most 60% of annotators, it is a *low agreement* pair.

The last measure, the *fraction of positive-labeled pairs*, is expected to be similar for different groups of annotators. Additionally, it provides information about the usefulness of the collected data, since a sizable fraction of positive examples is required to allow the development of algorithms which automatically detect claims mentioned in speeches.

4.1 Experts

The first group included highly proficient English-speakers with previous experience in various NLP annotation projects done by our team. Each speech was annotated by five experts.

This step was performed for two reasons: First, to verify that achieving high confidence annotation of our data is feasible, by comparing the annotation measures computed here to those reported in previous similar work which utilized experts. Second, establishing these measures for the experts group creates a baseline for comparison to the measures of crowd-based groups.

Results The *Experts* column of Table 1 summarizes the annotation statistics and results. The inter-annotator agreement of the experts group is 0.4, which is comparable yet somewhat lower, than the value of 0.52 reported in Mirkin et al. (2018). This could be attributed to the different nature of our claims, and having a more skewed data distribution: 20% of our claims are annotated as mentioned, while in the annotation of Mirkin et al. (2018) almost 40% of the claims are so.

4.2 General crowd

As mentioned above, despite having annotated a fairly large number of speech–claim pairs using experts, their limited pace, and the large volume of data, make it impractical to annotate the speeches en-masse in this way. We therefore resorted to the

	Experts	Crowd	Channel
Num. speeches	397	939	1127
Avg. claims per speech	22.8	27.3	65.6
Num. annotated pairs	9,052	25,634	73,931
Num. annotators	14	211	28
Avg. pairwise kappa	0.4	0.24	0.45
High-agreement pairs	80%	67%	68%
Low-agreement pairs	20%	15%	15%
Positive pairs	20%	17%	25%

Table 1: Speech-level annotation statistics (top) and results (bottom), comparing the use of 3 different groups of annotators. The crowd custom channel allowed the annotation of more than 7 times the amount of data annotated by experts, while maintaining quality.

use of the *Figure-Eight*[3] (F8) crowdsourcing platform.

This platform has several built-in quality control mechanisms. Each annotator has a *level*, based on her previous work on the platform. In addition, it encourages the use of *Test Questions* (TQs), questions whose answers are defined by the task's designer, and which are included in a preliminary quiz and in random locations throughout the task. The accuracy of each annotator is then measured on the TQs, and only those who maintain a high accuracy are assigned further questions (those who do not are denied access and their past work is discarded). While the annotators do not know which questions are TQs beforehand, once they submit their answers to one, the F8 platform reveals its correct answers. This allows annotators to review and learn from their mistakes, but also to recognize TQs after their answer was processed.

To create TQs for our task, speech–claim pairs that were unanimously labeled by the experts were taken, and their selected answer was defined as the correct answer. Recall that a question in our task is composed of a speech and a list of claims, and that one needs to answer, for each claim, whether it was mentioned in the speech. For TQs, we've set a known answer for only some of the claims on the list, and ignored answers to the rest. The annotators' minimal required accuracy was set to 0.75, and those with the lowest F8 *level* were denied access. Payment was set to $\$0.5$ per speech, and each question required seven annotators.

Results Column *Crowd* in Table 1 shows the agreement and quality measurements of this experiment. The obtained agreement is low compared to expert annotators. Such a significant difference is surprising given the TQ mechanism, which was expected to keep only annotators whose answers are consistent with those of the experts.

Analysis Analyzing the obtained annotations raised two major issues:

– *Implicit claims*: Focusing on high-agreement claim–speech pairs, 91% of the ones annotated by the crowd were labeled as negative, while the experts only annotated 37% of of their high-agreement pairs as such. A deeper look suggested that a major cause were claims alluded to, but not explicitly stated, in the speech (see Example 1). It seemed that while the experts generally agreed on these cases, the guidelines for the untrained crowd annotators did not fully convey the goal of this task. Thus, we changed the annotation labels for the task from binary to *Explicit*, *Implicit*, *No mention*, and added detailed examples of implicit mentions to the guidelines.

– *User reliability*: Further validation of a random sample of the data revealed many pairs for which, despite a high agreement, the label was wrong, thus raising concerns regarding the reliability of individual annotators. A possible explanation is that the TQs were identified by some annotators, who then made an effort to properly answer only them. This can happen, for example, when an annotator encounters the same TQ twice, or when annotators share answers to TQs with each other, if they are working as part of a group. While a possible solution is increasing the number of TQs to avoid such repetitions, it is still plausible, especially for returning annotators who work on multiple batches of the same task, to see the same TQ multiple times. Furthermore, it has been shown that in any quality assurance mechanism that is based on a fixed set of gold questions, the inherent size limit of the gold set can be exploited by a group of colluding workers, who can build an inferential system to detect which parts of the job are more likely to be gold questions (Checco et al., 2018).

4.3 Custom crowd

F8 allows manually defining a per-task list of annotators who are allowed access to a task, called a *custom channel*. To address the reliability issues raised in our analysis, annotators for such a channel were selected, based on the following per-

[3] `www.figure-eight.com` (formerly CrowdFlower).

annotator measures:
– ***Kappa***: Average pairwise kappa vs. others as described above.
– ***TQ failure***: Percentage of incorrectly labeled speech–claim pairs in TQs. This is a more refined assessment of the performance of individual annotators than the one provided by the platform, because the latter considers a TQ as wrong when it has at least one wrongly marked claim, and we assessed speech-claim pairs in TQs individually.
– ***Accept rate***: Percentage of positively annotated speech-claim pairs. Extreme values may suggest that an annotator is not reading carefully, and is rather choosing the same answer again and again.
– ***Judgment time***: Average annotation time of a speech. This is an estimate provided by the platform, and it helps to identify extreme outliers, which do not carefully review the task.
– ***Max pairwise kappa***: The maximal pairwise kappa measured between an annotator and one of her peers. A very high agreement between two annotators suggests that their answers may be coordinated. It may even be a single person, using different ids to access the same task multiple times.
– ***Shared IP***: Whether the annotator's IP address is shared with others doing the same task. Having the same IP address does not imply a single end-user, but it rasies the possibility that it is, or that the end-user is part of a group which may share answers to TQs.

Using these measures, each annotator is assigned a *Reliability Level*:
– **Unreliable**: Annotators who meet at least one of the following conditions: (i) *Accept rate* $< 5\%$ or $> 95\%$; (ii) *Max pairwise kappa* > 0.9; (iii) *Judgment time* < 1 minute; (iv) *shared IP* is true.
– **Low-Quality**: *Kappa* < 0.1 or *TQ failure* $> 50\%$. These are annotators with low quality of work but they are not necessarily malicious users.
– **Reliable**: the rest of the annotators.

The thresholds for the different reliability levels were manually defined after reviewing and analysing the annotation of workers comparing to their obtained scores.

To assess the reliability of the general crowd, these measures were calculated from their annotations, and a *Reliability Level* was assigned to each annotator. Of the 211 annotators who took part in that stage, only 86 were categorized as ***Reliable***. Of all 125 ***Unreliable*** annotators, 50 were also considered ***Low-Quality***. It is possible that the high rate of ***Unreliable*** annotators was due to the complexity of the task which discouraged serious and thorough work, combined with the high payment which attracted many annotators to try it.

We therefore hand-picked a group of ***Reliable*** annotators who contributed the largest number of high quality annotations to be included in a custom channel. By continuing to release in parallel more tasks to the general crowd, this channel was iteratively expanded, knowing such tasks will attract some ***Unreliable*** users, but also more ***Reliable*** ones. Once a task was complete, we calculated annotator levels, and picked new users from those identified as ***Reliable***. Answers from other annotators were discarded. At the same time, we released tasks limited to the custom channel, monitoring annotator performance using the same method.

Notably, when working with the custom channel we disabled the built-in TQ mechanism for two reasons. First, since channel annotators already proved reliable, the quiz given before each batch of the task was no longer necessary. Second, working with TQs technically requires including at least two speeches in every page of the task shown to the annotators (one speech being the TQ). Annotators pointed out that having this configuration makes it harder to focus.

To keep a measure of quality, one or two claims with a known clear answer were embedded as questions for each speech. For example, such a claim might be of a stance opposing that of the speaker, and is thus unlikely to be claimed. We refer to this quality measure as *Hidden Test Questions (HTQ)*, since in contrast to TQs, annotators can't identify them, and they don't know when they erred on them. Annotators only knew their work was closely monitored; and for our internal monitoring an ***HTQ failure*** measure replaces ***TQ failure*** when assessing the custom channel's work

Results After several iterations, we assembled a group of 28 annotators which achieved similar agreement to that of the expert annotators (see column *Channel* in Table 1), working at a much higher pace. This was probably due to the group including twice as many members as the expert annotators, as well as not being burdened with other annotation tasks (at least not by our team). To keep them motivated, we regularly paid bonuses to annotators based on the quantity and quality of their annotations. The annotators also provided occasional feedback on their experience which helped further improve the design of our task.

To demonstrate the resulting annotation, and to facilitate a basis for algorithms addressing this claim-detection task, an annotation of the speeches from Mirkin et al. (2018) will be made available on our website[4].

5 Comparing the annotations

Having constructed the speech-level annotated dataset, we now revisit our assumption that the simpler sentence-level annotation cannot capture the full context required to correctly label claims in speeches. We compare the annotation of 1,003 claims in 379 speeches via our speech-level methodology with that of the same claims via our initial sentence-level scheme. The latter was done on selected sentences from each speech - those semantically similar to the given claim (see §3).

Table 2 compares labels from both setups. Sentence-level labels are derived from 5,189 sentence–claim pairs (average of 1.7 sentences per speech-claim pair), considering a speech–claim pair positive if the claim was positive in at least one of the sentences annotated for this speech.

The rate of positive pairs is higher in the speech-level scheme: 1,024 pairs (20%) were labeled as positive (explicit or implicit) while only 389 (7.5%) were positive when deriving the label from the sentence-level scheme. As expected, the majority (74%) of sentence-level positives were also considered speech-level positive. Also, 28% of sentence-level negatives were in fact identified as speech-level *positives*, with a high rate of implicitly mentioned claims. Analyzing a sample of such cases suggested that usually the claim can not be pinpointed to a single sentence, but rather arises from a combination of several sentences, while it is also common for the sentence-level annotation to miss the relevant sentence, when one does exist.

Surprisingly, 102 pairs were labeled as positive in the sentence-level but were negative in the speech-level. This is unexpected because a claim that was mentioned in a single sentence of the speech was obviously mentioned in it. Analysis of these pairs revealed that in the majority of them (78%) the sentence-level label was wrong, that is, the claim was not mentioned in the suggested sentence. In many cases it seems that the mistake was due to misinterpretation of the sentence without its context. This confirms the importance of providing a broader context in our task.

[4]https://www.research.ibm.com/haifa/dept/vst/debating_data.shtml

Sent. \ Speech	Explicit	Implicit	No mention
Positive	150	137	102
Negative	301	436	1,889

Table 2: A comparison of speech-level labels (Explicit, Implicit, No mention) to sentence-level based labels: a Positive claim is one which is positive for least one of the labeled sentences; a Negative claim is one which is negative for all labeled sentences. Note that given a speech, not all of its sentences are labeled, leading to the label mismatches presented here. For further details, see §5.

6 Conclusions and Future Work

We addressed the annotation of claims in argumentative content through crowdsourcing. Due to its complexity, it is not clear that such annotation can be decomposed into simpler sub-tasks in a way that leads to an effective and comprehensive solution. Indeed, our results demonstrate that approximating the full-text context by simple *word2vec*-based sampling of ostensibly-relevant sentences is not sufficient.

Conversely, we show how careful employment of crowdsourcing can address the full, complex problem. By using a combination of various quality control measures to select highly skilled and motivated annotators, we were able to create a committed reliable workforce. This allowed us to obtain large-scale, high quality annotations despite the inherent complexity and subjectivity of this demanding NLU task. We learned that even with a relatively small group of crowd annotators, it is possible to benefit from the advantages of the crowd, namely high pace and scale.

We believe the key to the success of this annotation project was the ongoing learning and improvement we made during the process: analyzing common mistakes directed us to the easier 3-label setup, as well as improve the guidelines to clarify repeating issues and interesting edge cases; keeping an open dialog with our custom channel allowed us to learn from their feedback, and make changes that improved their experience like discarding the TQ mechanism; rewarding good annotators with extra payments made them feel their work is valued and kept them committed to our task.

In the context of more common NLU tasks, such as those in Wang et al. (2018), our task seems to require an exceptionally high level of language understanding by an automated system seeking to perform it. Since the claims may be implicit in the text, combining the understanding of numerous sentences may be required to perform it adequately. Moreover, if a claim is relevant to the motion, but nonetheless not mentioned in the speech, it may be quite challenging for an automatic system to deduce that such a plausible claim is in fact not implied anywhere in the speech. Hence this task is in line with the motivation of Wang et al. (2019) - a task where there is likely much headroom for an automated system to improve before it reaches human capabilities.

In future work, this dataset could be used to build classifiers of a more global nature, where each labeled speech–claim pair is considered a single unit of information.

Furthermore, speech-level annotation can help facilitate an efficient collection of claim–sentence labels, by first choosing claims labeled as positive in speeches, and annotating them against all speech sentences. Such labels may prove useful in the development of classifiers for identifying claims in single sentences. This method may be useful for other NLU tasks which involve long texts, e.g. Question Answering from long texts.

7 Acknowledgments

We thank George Taylor and the entire Figure-Eight team for their valuable advice and continuous support, which made this annotation project successful. We are thankful to all the debaters and annotators who took part in the creation of this dataset.

References

Alessandro Checco, Jo Bates, and Gianluca Demartini. 2018. All that glitters is goldan attack scheme on gold questions in crowdsourcing. In *Sixth AAAI Conference on Human Computation and Crowdsourcing*.

Eunsol Choi, He He, Mohit Iyyer, Mark Yatskar, Wen-tau Yih, Yejin Choi, Percy Liang, and Luke Zettlemoyer. 2018. Quac: Question answering in context. *arXiv preprint arXiv:1808.07036*.

Jacob Cohen. 1960. A Coefficient of Agreement for Nominal Scales. *Educational and Psychological Measurement*, 20(1):37–46.

Tim Finin, Will Murnane, Anand Karandikar, Nicholas Keller, Justin Martineau, and Mark Dredze. 2010. Annotating named entities in twitter data with crowdsourcing. In *Proceedings of the NAACL HLT 2010 Workshop on Creating Speech and Language Data with Amazon's Mechanical Turk*, CSLDAMT '10, pages 80–88, Stroudsburg, PA, USA. Association for Computational Linguistics.

Tanya Goyal, Tyler McDonnell, Mucahid Kutlu, Tamer Elsayed, and Matthew Lease. 2018. Your behavior signals your reliability: Modeling crowd behavioral traces to ensure quality relevance annotations. In *Sixth AAAI Conference on Human Computation and Crowdsourcing*.

Ivan Habernal and Iryna Gurevych. 2016. Which argument is more convincing? analyzing and predicting convincingness of web arguments using bidirectional lstm. In *Proceedings of the 54th Annual Meeting of the Association for Computational Linguistics (Volume 1: Long Papers)*, volume 1, pages 1589–1599.

Chien-Ju Ho, Shahin Jabbari, and Jennifer Wortman Vaughan. 2013. Adaptive task assignment for crowdsourced classification. In *International Conference on Machine Learning*, pages 534–542.

Tamar Lavee, Matan Orbach, Lili Kotlerman, Yoav Kantor, Shai Gretz, Lena Dankin, Shachar Mirkin, Michal Jacovi, Yonatan Bilu, Ranit Aharonov, and Noam Slonim. 2019. Towards effective rebuttal: Listening comprehension using corpus-wide claim mining. *6th Workshop on Argument Mining*.

Hongwei Li, Bo Zhao, and Ariel Fuxman. 2014. The wisdom of minority: Discovering and targeting the right group of workers for crowdsourcing. In *Proceedings of the 23rd International Conference on World Wide Web*, WWW '14, pages 165–176, New York, NY, USA. ACM.

Yashar Mehdad, Matteo Negri, and Marcello Federico. 2010. Towards cross-lingual textual entailment. In *Human Language Technologies: The 2010 Annual Conference of the North American Chapter of the Association for Computational Linguistics*, pages 321–324. Association for Computational Linguistics.

Tomas Mikolov, Kai Chen, Greg Corrado, and Jeffrey Dean. 2013. Efficient estimation of word representations in vector space. *CoRR*, abs/1301.3781.

Shachar Mirkin, Guy Moshkowich, Matan Orbach, Lili Kotlerman, Yoav Kantor, Tamar Lavee, Michal Jacovi, Yonatan Bilu, Ranit Aharonov, and Noam Slonim. 2018. Listening comprehension over argumentative content. In *Proceedings of the 2018 Conference on Empirical Methods in Natural Language Processing*, pages 719–724. Association for Computational Linguistics.

Matteo Negri, Luisa Bentivogli, Yashar Mehdad, Danilo Giampiccolo, and Alessandro Marchetti. 2011. Divide and conquer: Crowdsourcing the creation of cross-lingual textual entailment corpora. In *Proceedings of the Conference on Empirical Methods in Natural Language Processing*, pages 670–679. Association for Computational Linguistics.

Matan Orbach, Yonatan Bilu, Ariel Gera, Yoav Kantor, Lena Dankin, Tamar Lavee, Lili Kotlerman, Shachar Mirkin, Michal Jacovi, Ranit Aharonov, and Noam Slonim. 2019. A dataset of general-purpose rebuttal. In *Proceedings of the Conference on Empirical Methods in Natural Language Processing*. Association for Computational Linguistics.

Rebecca J Passonneau and Bob Carpenter. 2014. The benefits of a model of annotation. *Transactions of the Association for Computational Linguistics*, 2:311–326.

Pranav Rajpurkar, Robin Jia, and Percy Liang. 2018. Know what you don't know: Unanswerable questions for squad. *arXiv preprint arXiv:1806.03822*.

Pranav Rajpurkar, Jian Zhang, Konstantin Lopyrev, and Percy Liang. 2016. SQuAD: 100,000+ questions for machine comprehension of text. *arXiv preprint arXiv:1606.05250*.

Marta Sabou, Kalina Bontcheva, Leon Derczynski, and Arno Scharl. 2014. Corpus annotation through crowdsourcing: Towards best practice guidelines. In *LREC*, pages 859–866.

Merel Scholman and Vera Demberg. 2017. Crowdsourcing discourse interpretations: On the influence of context and the reliability of a connective insertion task. In *Proceedings of the 11th Linguistic Annotation Workshop*, pages 24–33, Valencia, Spain. Association for Computational Linguistics.

Alex Wang, Yada Pruksachatkun, Nikita Nangia, Amanpreet Singh, Julian Michael, Felix Hill, Omer Levy, and Samuel R Bowman. 2019. Superglue: A stickier benchmark for general-purpose language understanding systems. *arXiv preprint arXiv:1905.00537*.

Alex Wang, Amanpreet Singh, Julian Michael, Felix Hill, Omer Levy, and Samuel R. Bowman. 2018. GLUE: A multi-task benchmark and analysis platform for natural language understanding. In *Proceedings of the Workshop: Analyzing and Interpreting Neural Networks for NLP, BlackboxNLP@EMNLP 2018, Brussels, Belgium, November 1, 2018*, pages 353–355.

Aobo Wang, Cong Duy Vu Hoang, and Min-Yen Kan. 2013. Perspectives on crowdsourcing annotations for natural language processing. *Language resources and evaluation*, 47(1):9–31.

Rui Wang and Chris Callison-Burch. 2010. Cheap facts and counter-facts. In *Proceedings of the NAACL HLT 2010 Workshop on Creating Speech and Language Data with Amazons Mechanical Turk*, pages 163–167.

Naomi Zeichner, Jonathan Berant, and Ido Dagan. 2012. Crowdsourcing inference-rule evaluation. In *Proceedings of the 50th Annual Meeting of the Association for Computational Linguistics: Short Papers-Volume 2*, pages 156–160. Association for Computational Linguistics.

Computer Assisted Annotation of Tension Development in TED Talks through Crowdsourcing

Seungwon Yoon **Wonsuk Yang** **Jong C. Park**[†]
School of Computing
Korea Advanced Institute of Science and Technology
{swyoon, derrick0511, park}@nlp.kaist.ac.kr

Abstract

We propose a method of machine-assisted annotation for the identification of tension development, annotating whether the tension is increasing, decreasing, or staying unchanged. We use a neural network based prediction model, whose predicted results are given to the annotators as initial values for the options that they are asked to choose. By presenting such initial values to the annotators, the annotation task becomes an evaluation task where the annotators inspect whether or not the predicted results are correct. To demonstrate the effectiveness of our method, we performed the annotation task in both in-house and crowdsourced environments. For the crowdsourced environment, we compared the annotation results with and without our method of machine-assisted annotation. We find that the results with our method showed a higher agreement to the gold standard than those without, though our method had little effect at reducing the time for annotation. Our codes for the experiment are made publicly available[1].

1 Introduction

Recently, researchers for natural language processing are paying more attention to crowdsourcing for its effectiveness in linguistic annotations. The recent development in crowdsourcing platforms such as Amazon Mechanical Turk (AMT) has much reduced the time and effort required for an annotation project. Many researchers proposed methods to assist the workers in the crowdsourced annotation (Yuen et al. (2011); Poesio et al. (2013); Guillaume et al. (2016); Madge et al. (2019); Yang et al. (2019)). In particular, Guillaume et al. (2016) designed a game-based platform for the annotation of dependency relations in French text, with the prediction model embedded in their platform. Yang et al. (2019) proposed to predict the difficulty of an annotation unit in order to allocate relatively easy units to crowdsourcing workers and the rest to expert annotators.

In this paper, we present a machine-assisting method for effective annotation of tension development. Tension is a means to keep the attention of the reader or audience, studied mainly in the field of storytelling (Zillmann (1980); Klimmt et al. (2009); Niehaus and Young (2014)). Tension also plays a critical role in discourse development (Lehne and Koelsch, 2015). We annotate the tension development, whether the tension is increasing, decreasing, or staying unchanged, in the TED Talks. We also introduce a Self-Assessment Manikin (SAM), which is an intuitive diagram that helps understand the annotation guidelines for tension annotation. Our method uses a prediction model for tension development, and provides the annotators with model predicted results as initial values. The predictions are based on the audio, the subtitle of the given video clip and the previous annotation results by an annotator.

We validate our method through an experiment on crowdsourced annotations. The annotations with our method show a higher agreement to the gold standard, which we instructed manually by annotating independently from the crowdsourced annotations, than those without our method. However, contrary to our initial expectation that our method will also reduce the annotation time, we find that it hardly reduced the time.

The contributions of this paper are as follows. (1) We proposed a new annotation scheme using the Self-Assessment Manikin (SAM) to annotate the tension development on multimodal data. (2) To the best our knowledge, our method is the first in utilizing a prediction model to assist the annotation of tension development. We show experimen-

[†] Corresponding author

[1] https://github.com/nlpcl-lab/ted-talks-annotation

Proceedings of the First Workshop on Aggregating and Analysing Crowdsourced Annotations for NLP, pages 39–47
Hong Kong, China, November 3, 2019. ©2019 Association for Computational Linguistics
https://doi.org/10.18653/v1/P17

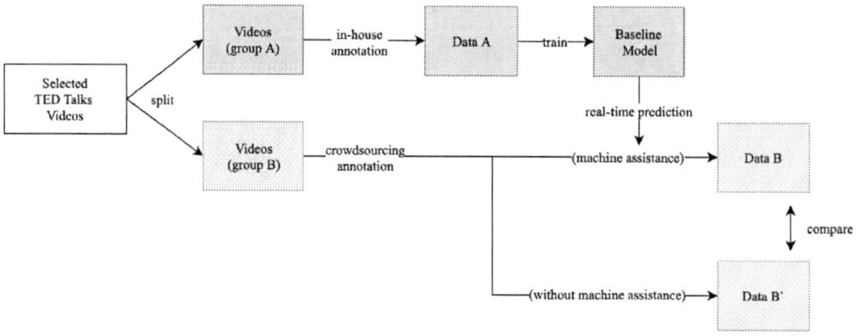

Figure 1: Overview of the annotation process

tally that our method is effective at gathering high-quality data and provide a detailed analysis of the annotation results. (3) We make the related data and the code publicly available.

2 Related work

2.1 Computer-Assisted Annotation

Ringger et al. (2008) suggested a machine-assisted method for part-of-speech (POS) tagging. They provided model predicted results to the annotators so that the annotators may focus only on incorrect predictions. There has been a line of researches for effective visualization and an improvement on the user-interface that can help a linguistic annotation process (Stenetorp et al. (2012); Yimam et al. (2013)). Guillaume et al. (2016) provided a game-based platform for the annotation of dependency relations in French text and used a prediction model as a part of the platform in the training phase for the annotators before the main data gathering. For the selection of the target data to annotate, active learning has been employed to selectively collect only the training data on which the model does not perform well in order to maximize the performance of the model with a dataset that is as small as possible (Wang et al. (2017); Duong et al. (2018)). Schulz et al. (2019) showed that the provision of the automatically generated annotation results can accelerate the annotation process and enhance the annotation quality, without incurring a significant bias.

For visual object detection, Yao et al. (2012) presented an annotation platform that contains a prediction model for the location of the given object. In their platform, the model presents the predicted location to the annotators, and the annotators modified the location if it is incorrect. They also predicted the time that the annotator may take for the modification and presented the annotation unit to the annotators with the shortest expected time to minimize the total cost of their annotation project. Su et al. (2012) presented a quantification test that can identify the annotators who do not fully understand the annotation guidelines. They also presented a rule-based feedback system that can warn untrained annotators before continuing the annotation.

2.2 Emotion, suspense, and tension

Tension is a psychological concept that is related to emotion and suspense. Tension has been studied along with suspense for the literature, movies, and games (Brewer and Lichtenstein (1982); Zillmann (1980); Klimmt et al. (2009)). Lehne and Koelsch (2015) proposed a general psychological model for tension without any further restriction on its domain, defining the magnitude of tension as the interval between positive and negative expectations of the outcome.

In the field of computer science, there has been a line of researches modeling the mental state of the reader to create an intense story (Niehaus and Young (2014); O'Neill and Riedl (2014)). Li et al. (2018) designed a scheme for story structures considering dramatic tension changes and the narrative structure suggested by Helm and MacNeish (1967) and annotated the story structure for short stories and personal anecdotes. For the analysis of emotion, Cowie and Sawey (2011) annotated on the intensity of laughter and the degree of positive emotion in the videos of babies. Metallinou and Narayanan (2013) annotated on activation, valence, and dominance with an assumption that the three attributes represent the state of emotion in video. Antony et al. (2014) annotated changes in

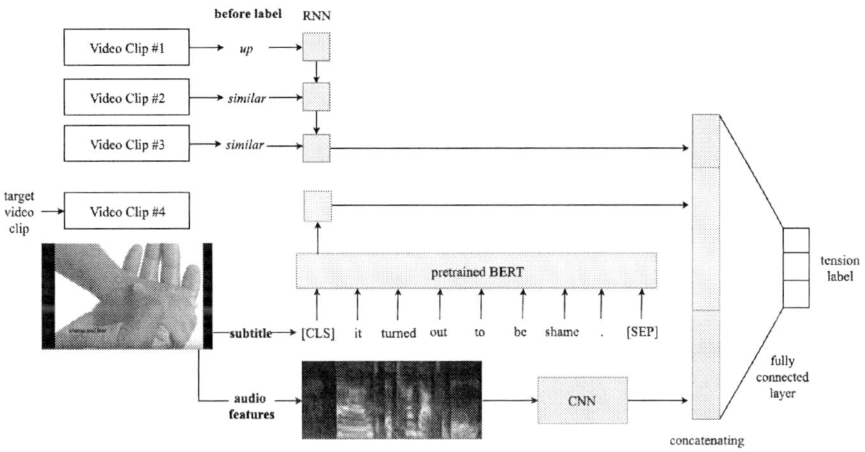

Figure 2: Model architecture

arousal and valence with heart rate, electrodermal activity, and respiration rate. The multi-modal data collection enables a more flexible analysis of the environmental interactions.

3 Data

We used the TED Talks as a dataset to track the tension development. TED Talks are a conference that presents ideas on various topics in a few minutes, and the video part has been used for emotional analysis and assessment of engagement exploiting the highly reliable English subtitles precisely synchronized to the video (Neumann and Vu (2019); Haider et al. (2017)). For the annotation of tension development, we have chosen to use TED Talks with two specific reasons: (1) Due to the nature of public lectures, many utterances raise the tension to keep the attention of the audience. (2) The applause or laughter of the audience, which may be highly related to tension development, is also recorded in the video.

In the archives of TED Talks[2], we randomly selected 20 videos whose running time is in the range of 10-20 minutes. For each of the 20 videos, we divided it into a set of small video clips, where the division was based on the subtitles so that a clip corresponds to a sentence. The English subtitles were split into sentences. We obtained a dataset containing 3,597 video clips with a total duration of 301 minutes. Each sentence that corresponds to a video clip consists of 14 words on average.

4 Method

Our method uses a neural network based prediction model, and provides the predicted results to the annotators as the initial values for the options that the annotator is asked to fill out. By this, the annotation task, originally to choose the correct label for a given video clip, is transformed into an evaluation task, judging whether or not the predicted result by the model is correct.

Figure 2 shows the architecture of our model. The model predicts the label for each video clip sequentially, and utilizes three features: subtitles, audio, and the formerly chosen labels for the previous video clips. The audio of a video clip was encoded into a vector using CNN. We used pyAudioAnalysis software (Giannakopoulos, 2015) to extract 34 features such as MFCC at the rate of 30 frames/sec, and the features were passed to the CNN. The CNN consists of three 1D convolutional layers. 1D max-pooling with ReLU activation function is performed after each convolutional layer. The lecture's subtitles were encoded into a vector using a pre-trained uncased BERT-base model (Devlin et al., 2019). The previously chosen k labels were encoded into a vector using an RNN. The three vectors for the three features were concatenated into a vector, passed afterwards to the output layer, or the fully connected layer.

[2]Videos and subtitles at http://www.ted.com are publicly available under Creative Commons license, Attribution–Non Commercial–No Derivatives.

type	#videos	#video clips
in-house	10 (group A)	1,736
crowdsourced	10 (group B)	1,861
all	20	3,597

Table 1: Statistics of the data

label (score)	guidelines
up (+1)	Watch the video clip and select *up* if your feeling matches one of the pictures below.  **interesting**: I'm interested, want to learn more and know what's next. **thinking**: I'm thinking about the content of the lecture (e.g., when the speaker asks a question). **surprised**: I'm surprised at seeing something I didn't expect. **annoyed**: I'm uncomfortable or feeling that the content is unpleasant or difficult to agree with. **confused**: I'm confused because it is different from what I originally knew or it is difficult to understand.
down (-1)	Watch the video clip and select *down* if your feeling matches one of the pictures below.  **relieved**: I am comfortable again, due to the removal of any previous anxiety or doubt. **funny**: I find the speaker's joke(s) or content to be amusing. **boring**: I am not interested in the repetition of similar and/or uninteresting content.
similar (0)	Watch the video clip and select *similar* when your status is neither *up* nor *down*. If you are uncertain about your feeling, as shown in the third video clip of the picture below, select *similar*. 

Table 2: Annotation guidelines for the change in tension

5 Annotation

5.1 Overview

Figure 1 gives an overview of our annotation of tension development. First, as shown in Table 1, 10 TED Talks videos were divided into group A and group B. In-house annotation was performed on group A and the results, which we call data A, were used for training the prediction model. Then, group B was annotated through Amazon Mechanical Turk (AMT), a crowdsourcing platform. For group B, the crowdsourced annotation was conducted in two phases. First, every video in group B was annotated via AMT *using* our method (data B). Second, independently of the first, every video in group B was annotated via AMT, *not using* our method (data B′).

For a video, the annotators watched the video clips in their original order, and annotated on each clip with one of the three labels, *up*, *down*, and *similar*. *Up* indicates that the tension is increasing, and *down* indicates that it is decreasing. *Similar* indicates that the tension is not changing. As it is disruptive for the annotator to iterate the clicking on the video for playing and pausing, we made an annotation tool to prevent such disruption (Figure 3).

Due to the copyright issue, we could not post the TED Talks video directly online. Instead, we provided the annotators, or crowdsourcing workers, with the videos at TED's official Youtube channel[3] via an embedded player, controlled by the APIs provided by the Youtube player. If the annotator enters a shortcut key to move to the next video clip or presses the play button of the video clip, the video clip is played. After the video clip meets the end (of the clip), an input window for annotation is displayed. Then, the annotator can perform the annotation on the clip, and proceed to the next clip. We also provided the subtitles explicitly to the annotators.

5.2 Annotation Scheme

The tension development within each video clip was annotated with one of the three values (*up*, *down*, or *similar*). We defined each of the three labels based on the specific circumstances in Table 2. Five circumstances, which are interesting,

[3]`https://www.youtube.com/user/TEDtalksDirector`

[4]source of the video: `https://www.youtube.com/watch?v=iCvmsMzlF7o`

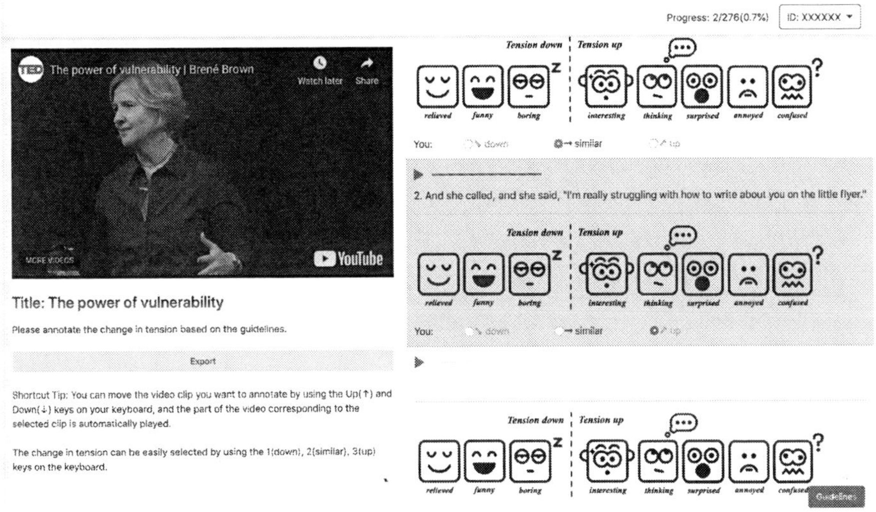

Figure 3: Interface of the annotation tool[4]

thinking, surprised, annoyed, and confused, correspond to *up*. If a video clip can be described as one of the five circumstances, we defined the video clip to have the label of *up*. In a similar way, three circumstances, or relieved, funny, and boring, correspond to the label of *down*. If a video clip is judged to be neither *up* nor *down*, we defined it as having the label of *similar*. It should be noted that the definition of the labels is designed specifically for the domain of public lectures. For example, ridiculing someone in everyday life may increase the tension. Still, in lectures, it is often intended to help the audience to feel relaxed and help them to feel comfortable listening (Meyer, 2000). Therefore, we set it as a circumstance for *down*.

To help the annotators to intuitively follow up the annotation guidelines, and for the cases where the annotators forget the details of the guidelines (of the specification of the circumstances), we provided Self-Assessment Manikins (SAMs) to the annotators as shown in Table 2. Providing SAMs to annotators has been acknowledged to be an effective method for an emotion-related annotation task (Bradley and Lang (1994); Yadati et al. (2013); Boccignone et al. (2017)).

5.3 Annotation Procedure

5.3.1 In-house Annotation

The in-house annotation method was used to annotate 1,736 video clips (group A). A total of five annotators participated, and three annotators annotated the video clips for each video. 5,208 annotation values were obtained for 10 videos containing 1,736 video clips. The distribution of *down*, *similar*, and *up* labels was 749 (14.4%), 3,218 (61.8%), and 1,239 (23.8%), respectively.

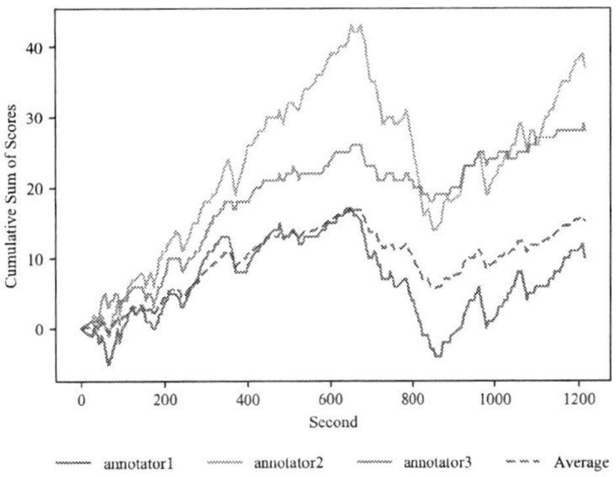

Figure 4: Example of annotations by three annotators

Figure 4 illustrates an example of the cumulative sum of scores annotated by three annotators for the same video. The chosen values were slightly different among the annotators (Krippendorff's α: 0.298), but the tendency to exceed or fall short of the cumulative sum of scores was similar (mean correlation: 0.73). Since each annotator has a different personal scale by which to rate emotion, Pearson's correlation and Cronbach's α, which are indicators that focus on trends when evaluating the agreement of annotation,

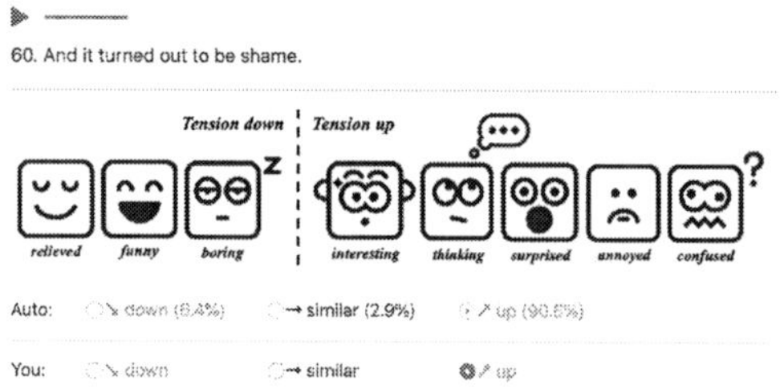

Figure 5: Interface showing predicted values in machine-assisted annotation

were used (McKeown et al. (2011); Metallinou and Narayanan (2013)). For in-house annotations, we obtained the agreements as shown in Table 5. Pearson's correlation and Cronbach's α were measured as the cumulative sum of the scores.

type	down	similar	up	sum
train	153	819	243	1,215
test	69	342	110	521
all	222	1,161	353	1,736

Table 3: Statistics of the data for training the model

5.3.2 Crowdsourcing Annotation

Of the data collected via in-house annotations to the Group A videos, 70% were used as the training set and 30% were used as the test set to train and evaluate the model (Table 3). When setting the ground truth from data annotated by three people in the same video clip, we decided to use majority voting among *down*, *similar*, and *up* labels. If each label was selected once, the label *similar* was set as the ground truth.

When annotating with crowdsourcing, the videos in group B were annotated with and without machine assistance by three annotators each (Figure 5). Video clips annotated without machine assistance were annotated using the same interface as used for the in-house annotation. During machine-assisted annotation, predicted values by the model are presented along with the probability, and the label with the highest probability was given to the annotator as the default value. The trained model provided predicted values in real-time using the subtitles, sound of the video clips and the tension values that the user annotated in the previous five video clips. Annotators were instructed to refer to the automatic prediction value:

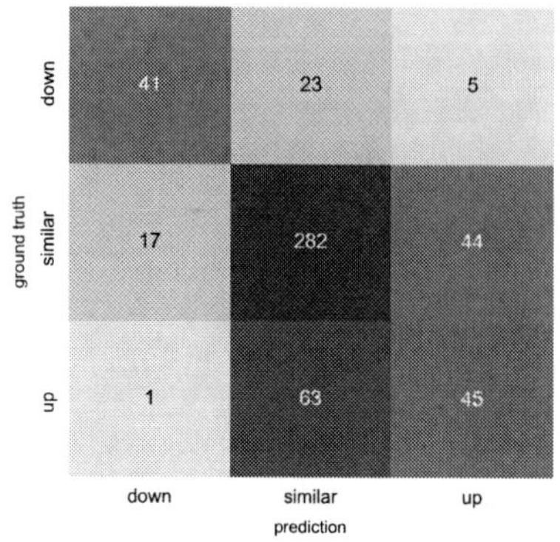

Figure 6: Confusion matrix of the prediction model on the test set

"Please note that the value of the predicted tension is automatically given as the default value. If your judgment is different, change the value according to your judgment. If the default value matches your judgment, you may move on to the next video clip."

We used the Amazon Mechanical Turk (AMT) service for crowdsourcing, providing workers with annotation guidelines and the URL for the web-based annotation tool. Each worker was allowed to participate in annotating several different videos. Workers with the number of HITs approved > 50 and HIT approval rate $> 95\%$ were allowed to join. There were a total of 47 annotators.

feature	Precision	Recall	F1
audio	0.54	0.50	0.52
text	0.61	0.60	0.60
before label (k=5)	0.43	0.49	0.45
audio + text + before label (k=5)	0.65	0.61	0.63

Table 4: Comparison of the performance on the test set according to the features used

5.3.3 Analysis of Annotations

Figure 6 shows the confusion matrix of the prediction model in the test set. The performance (F1 score) for the down label (0.64) was higher than that for up (0.44). Table 4 compares the performance according to the features used. The performance was lowest when the tension labels of the previous video clip were used as a feature. It was highest when they used three types of features together.

type		video group	#annotator for each video clip	agreement			mean selection time (seconds)
				mean Pearson's correlation	mean Cronbach's α	Krippendorff's α	
in-house		group A	3	0.645	0.855	0.283	2.02
crowdsourced	machine assistance	group B	3	0.817	0.817	0.387	2.61
	no machine assistance	group B	3	0.636	0.469	0.134	2.69

Table 5: Statistics for agreement, time of annotation results

As the result of the annotation, 11,166 annotation values were obtained for 10 videos with 1,861 video clips (group B). For machine-assisted annotations, the distribution of *down*, *similar* and *up* was 895 (16.0%), 2,862 (51.3%), and 1,826 (32.7%), respectively. For unassisted annotations from the machine, the distribution was 977 (17.5%), 2,372 (42.4%), and 2,232 (39.9%). Table 5 shows the agreement among the annotation results. In-house annotations were all higher in all the three metric than the crowdsourced annotations without machine-assistance. In the control group, machine-assisted annotations showed higher levels of agreement than non-assisted annotations.

We analyzed whether the improvement of agreement rate was a negative effect from the bias resulting from the predicted labels. For analysis, gold labels were compared to annotations. Gold labels were set by the annotations of one of the authors with no machine assistance in 4 videos selected in group B. Figure 7 shows an example of such gold labels, machine-assisted annotations and the annotations of the control group for the cumulative sum of the tension score. Comparing the mean correlation for the 4 videos, the mean correlation of the machine-assisted annotations was 0.861, higher than the control group's mean correlation of 0.466. The annotation values were more in line with the trend among gold labels with machine-assistance.

The mean correlation between machine predictions itself and gold labels was 0.867. This means that machine-assisted annotators can achieve results closer to gold than the control group if they accept all the predicted values. However, machine-assisted annotators changed 26.5% of the labels presented as default values through the model (Figure 8). The change ratio of prediction values for each of *down*, *similar* and *up* is 17.7%, 28.8% and 24.3%, respectively. This produced a difference between machine predictions and machine-assisted annotations, as illustrated in Figure 7. The

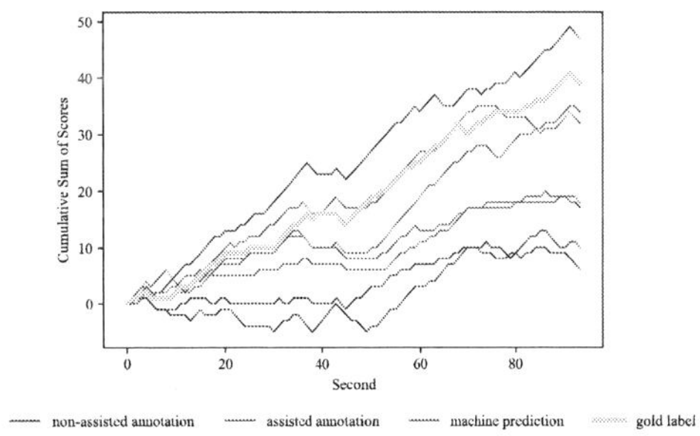

Figure 7: Example of annotations with gold label

average of the probabilities (as shown in Figure 5) presented with labels set as default values by the prediction model was 90.4%. When the user changed the default value, the average of the probabilities was 87.0%. When the user did not change the default value, the average was 91.6%.

The selection times in Table 5 represent the amount of time it takes to select the tension label from the time the video clip is played to the end. For machine-assisted annotations, if the default value is not changed by the annotator, the time between the end of the current video clip and the start of the next video clip was considered as the selection time. When receiving machine assistance, the annotation time was expected to be reduced because the input process of selecting labels would disappear if the model prediction values and the annotator's judgments were the same. However, there was no significant difference compared to the control group.

6 Conclusion

In this paper, we introduced a method for machine-assisted annotation of tension development. Our method utilizes a prediction model to provide the predicted result to the annotators so that the annotation task is turned into an evaluation task of inspecting whether or not the prediction by the model is correct. We find that our method enhances the agreement of the crowdsourced anno-

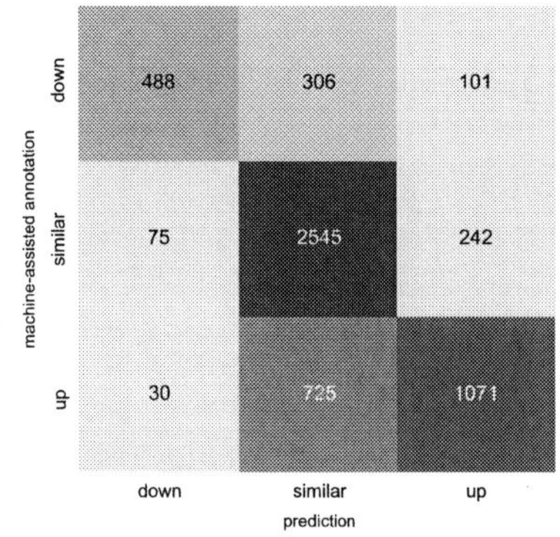

Figure 8: Confusion matrix of the prediction model on the group B videos

tations to the gold standard annotation in a small trial of 3 annotators. We also find that our method does not particularly affect the time taken for the annotation.

We proposed a new annotation scheme using the Self-Assessment Manikin (SAM) to annotate the tension development. By converting the annotation task into a verification task via machine assistance, the results become consequently more aligned with the gold standard compared with the control group.

Acknowledgments

This work was supported by Institute for Information and communications Technology Promotion (IITP) grant funded by the Korea government (MSIT) (No. 2018-0-00582-002, Prediction and augmentation of the credibility distribution via linguistic analysis and automated evidence document collection). We thank the anonymous reviewers for the much helpful feedback.

References

J Antony, K Sharma, C Castellini, Egon L van den Broek, and C Borst. 2014. Continuous affect state annotation using a joystick-based user interface. In *Proceedings of Measuring Behavior*, pages 268–271.

Giuseppe Boccignone, Donatello Conte, Vittorio Cuculo, and Raffaella Lanzarotti. 2017. Amhuse: a multimodal dataset for humour sensing. In *Proceedings of the 19th ACM International Conference on Multimodal Interaction*, pages 438–445. ACM.

Margaret M Bradley and Peter J Lang. 1994. Measuring emotion: the self-assessment manikin and the semantic differential. *Journal of behavior therapy and experimental psychiatry*, 25(1):49–59.

William F Brewer and Edward H Lichtenstein. 1982. Stories are to entertain: A structural-affect theory of stories. *Journal of pragmatics*, 6(5-6):473–486.

Roddy Cowie and Martin Sawey. 2011. Gtrace-general trace program from queen's, belfast. Https://sites.google.com/site/roddycowie/work-resources.

Jacob Devlin, Ming-Wei Chang, Kenton Lee, and Kristina Toutanova. 2019. BERT: Pre-training of deep bidirectional transformers for language understanding. In *Proceedings of the 2019 Conference of the North American Chapter of the Association for Computational Linguistics: Human Language Technologies, Volume 1 (Long and Short Papers)*, pages 4171–4186, Minneapolis, Minnesota. Association for Computational Linguistics.

Long Duong, Hadi Afshar, Dominique Estival, Glen Pink, Philip Cohen, and Mark Johnson. 2018. Active learning for deep semantic parsing. In *Proceedings of the 56th Annual Meeting of the Association for Computational Linguistics (Volume 2: Short Papers)*, pages 43–48.

Theodoros Giannakopoulos. 2015. pyaudioanalysis: An open-source python library for audio signal analysis. *PloS one*, 10(12):e0144610.

Bruno Guillaume, Karën Fort, and Nicolas Lefebvre. 2016. Crowdsourcing complex language resources: Playing to annotate dependency syntax. In *Proceedings of the International Conference on Computational Linguistics (COLING)*.

Fasih Haider, Fahim A Salim, Saturnino Luz, Carl Vogel, Owen Conlan, and Nick Campbell. 2017. Visual, laughter, applause and spoken expression features for predicting engagement within TED talks. *Feedback*, 10:20.

June Helm and June Helm MacNeish. 1967. *Essays on the verbal and visual arts*. University of Washington Press.

Christoph Klimmt, Albert Rizzo, Peter Vorderer, Jan Koch, and Till Fischer. 2009. Experimental evidence for suspense as determinant of video game enjoyment. *CyberPsychology & Behavior*, 12(1):29–31.

Moritz Lehne and Stefan Koelsch. 2015. Toward a general psychological model of tension and suspense. *Frontiers in Psychology*, 6:79.

Boyang Li, Beth Cardier, Tong Wang, and Florian Metze. 2018. Annotating high-level structures of short stories and personal anecdotes. In *Proceedings of the Eleventh International Conference on Language Resources and Evaluation (LREC-2018)*, Miyazaki, Japan. European Languages Resources Association (ELRA).

Chris Madge, Juntao Yu, Jon Chamberlain, Udo Kruschwitz, Silviu Paun, and Massimo Poesio. 2019. Crowdsourcing and aggregating nested markable annotations. In *Proceedings of the 57th Conference of the Association for Computational Linguistics*, pages 797–807.

Gary McKeown, Michel Valstar, Roddy Cowie, Maja Pantic, and Marc Schroder. 2011. The semaine database: Annotated multimodal records of emotionally colored conversations between a person and a limited agent. *IEEE Transactions on Affective Computing*, 3(1):5–17.

Angeliki Metallinou and Shrikanth Narayanan. 2013. Annotation and processing of continuous emotional attributes: Challenges and opportunities. In *2013 10th IEEE international conference and workshops on automatic face and gesture recognition (FG)*, pages 1–8. IEEE.

John C Meyer. 2000. Humor as a double-edged sword: Four functions of humor in communication. *Communication theory*, 10(3):310–331.

Michael Neumann and Ngoc Thang Vu. 2019. Improving speech emotion recognition with unsupervised representation learning on unlabeled speech. In *IEEE International Conference on Acoustics, Speech and Signal Processing (ICASSP)*, pages 7390–7394. IEEE.

James Niehaus and R Michael Young. 2014. Cognitive models of discourse comprehension for narrative generation. *Literary and linguistic computing*, 29(4):561–582.

Brian O'Neill and Mark Riedl. 2014. Dramatis: A computational model of suspense. In *28th AAAI Conference on Artificial Intelligence*, pages 944–950.

Massimo Poesio, Jon Chamberlain, Udo Kruschwitz, Livio Robaldo, and Luca Ducceschi. 2013. Phrase detectives: Utilizing collective intelligence for internet-scale language resource creation. *ACM Transactions on Interactive Intelligent Systems (TiiS)*, 3(1):3.

Eric K Ringger, Marc Carmen, Robbie Haertel, Kevin D Seppi, Deryle Lonsdale, Peter McClanahan, James L Carroll, and Noel Ellison. 2008. Assessing the costs of machine-assisted corpus annotation through a user study. In *Proceedings of LREC*, volume 8, pages 3318–3324.

Claudia Schulz, Christian M. Meyer, Jan Kiesewetter, Michael Sailer, Elisabeth Bauer, Martin R. Fischer, Frank Fischer, and Iryna Gurevych. 2019. Analysis of automatic annotation suggestions for hard discourse-level tasks in expert domains. In *Proceedings of the 57th Annual Meeting of the Association for Computational Linguistics*, pages 2761–2772, Florence, Italy. ACL.

Pontus Stenetorp, Sampo Pyysalo, Goran Topić, Tomoko Ohta, Sophia Ananiadou, and Jun'ichi Tsujii. 2012. Brat: a web-based tool for nlp-assisted text annotation. In *Proceedings of the Demonstrations at the 13th Conference of the European Chapter of the Association for Computational Linguistics*, pages 102–107. ACL.

Hao Su, Jia Deng, and Li Fei-Fei. 2012. Crowdsourcing annotations for visual object detection. In *Workshops at the 26th AAAI Conference on Artificial Intelligence*.

Chenguang Wang, Laura Chiticariu, and Yunyao Li. 2017. Active learning for black-box semantic role labeling with neural factors. In *Proceedings of IJCAI*, pages 2908–2914.

Karthik Yadati, Harish Katti, and Mohan Kankanhalli. 2013. Cavva: Computational affective video-in-video advertising. *IEEE Transactions on Multimedia*, 16(1):15–23.

Yinfei Yang, Oshin Agarwal, Chris Tar, Byron C. Wallace, and Ani Nenkova. 2019. Predicting annotation difficulty to improve task routing and model performance for biomedical information extraction. In *Proceedings of the 2019 Conference of the North American Chapter of the Association for Computational Linguistics: Human Language Technologies, Volume 1 (Long and Short Papers)*, pages 1471–1480, Minneapolis, Minnesota. ACL.

Angela Yao, Juergen Gall, Christian Leistner, and Luc Van Gool. 2012. Interactive object detection. In *Proceedings of IEEE Conference on Computer Vision and Pattern Recognition*, pages 3242–3249. IEEE.

Seid Muhie Yimam, Iryna Gurevych, Richard Eckart de Castilho, and Chris Biemann. 2013. Webanno: A flexible, web-based and visually supported system for distributed annotations. In *Proceedings of the 51st Annual Meeting of the Association for Computational Linguistics: System Demonstrations*, pages 1–6.

Man-Ching Yuen, Irwin King, and Kwong-Sak Leung. 2011. A survey of crowdsourcing systems. In *Proceedings of IEEE Third International Conference on Privacy, Security, Risk and Trust and IEEE Third International Conference on Social Computing*, pages 766–773. IEEE.

Dolf Zillmann. 1980. Anatomy of suspense. In *The entertainment functions of television*, pages 133–163. Hillsdale, NJ: Erlbaum.

CoSSAT: Code-Switched Speech Annotation Tool

Sanket Shah **Pratik Joshi** **Sebastin Santy** **Sunayana Sitaram**
Microsoft Research, Bangalore, India
{t-sansha, t-prjos, t-sesan, susitara}@microsoft.com

Abstract

Code-switching refers to the alternation of two or more languages in a conversation or utterance and is common in multilingual communities across the world. Building code-switched speech and natural language processing systems are challenging due to the lack of annotated speech and text data. We present a speech annotation interface CoSSAT, which helps annotators transcribe code-switched speech faster, more easily and more accurately than a traditional interface, by displaying candidate words from monolingual speech recognizers. We conduct a user study on the transcription of Hindi-English code-switched speech with 10 annotators and describe quantitative and qualitative results.

1 Introduction

Code-switching is a phenomenon that occurs in multilingual societies wherein speakers who are fluent in two or more languages switch between these languages in the same conversation or an utterance. Code-switching is a challenging problem for speech and natural language processing systems to handle due to the lack of manually annotated data and resources. However, due to the ubiquitous nature of code-switching in speech and text produced by multilingual speakers, it is an important problem for speech and NLP systems to tackle.

Automatic Speech Recognition (ASR) is used by a variety of systems to convert speech to text for further processing. Deep Neural Network (DNN) based systems have increased the accuracy of ASR systems to match human-level performance. However, these gains are only obtained in high-resource languages that have thousands of hours of manually transcribed speech data. Code-switched languages suffer from a lack of manually annotated training data, as described in (Sitaram et al., 2019), with the largest publicly available speech corpus in Mandarin-English being 63 hours long (Lyu et al., 2015).

In cases where the two languages being mixed are in different scripts, the transcriber needs to switch between two scripts while annotating an utterance. This paper introduces an interface which assists in the transcription of code-switched Hindi-English speech data by displaying candidate words generated by monolingual Hindi and English speech recognizers, without the need for a code-switched ASR. We present quantitative and qualitative results from a user study with 10 users who use our proposed interface as well as a traditional typing-only interface for transcribing code-switched speech.

2 Related Work

Using hypotheses produced by an ASR system is a common approach used to reduce human effort in transcribing speech (Sperber et al., 2016). However, this approach often induces a bias amongst the annotators while transcribing text (Levit et al., 2017). To mitigate this bias, we do not provide the hypothesis as a suggested transcription, but rather provide a collection of suggested words for the annotators to choose from. We leverage a combination of monolingual ASRs rather than a code-switched ASR for our task. Our work is inspired by efforts in Spoken Term Detection (STD) for Hindi-English code-switched speech, in which (Shah and Sitaram, 2019) use post-processing techniques to improve hypothesis produced by monolingual ASR for code-switched speech. Similarly for Chinese-English code-switched speech, (Shan-Ruei You et al., 2004) combine scores from monolingual Chinese and English ASRs to determine the most probable output. In contrast, for this work, we neither determine a single combined

Proceedings of the First Workshop on Aggregating and Analysing Crowdsourced Annotations for NLP, pages 48–52
Hong Kong, China, November 3, 2019. ©2019 Association for Computational Linguistics
https://doi.org/10.18653/v1/P17

ASR hypothesis nor do any post-processing on the ASR hypothesis, but rather use the output of the two recognizers to display candidate words for annotation purposes.

3 Methodology

Given a speech utterance, we generate an ordered sequence of candidate code-switched words using monolingual speech recognizers. Our method consists of two main steps, (1) Dynamic Audio Segmentation, (2) Combining ASR hypotheses.

3.1 Dynamic Audio Segmentation

Due to the low accuracy of the monolingual speech recognizers on code-switched input, it is important to find segments in the audio where the monolingual recognizers have high confidence. To enable this, we automatically segment the audio according to ASR confidence. This audio segmentation task can be formulated as an optimization problem for a given set of possible boundaries. We try to optimize the segment size based on the confidence scores of the monolingual ASRs on code-switched speech. We start with a segment of size 0.5 seconds from the beginning of the audio, and pass this audio segment through the monolingual Hindi and English ASRs. Each ASR provides an utterance (or audio chunk, in this case) level confidence value in the range of 0-1.

If the confidence values given by both recognizers are less than 0.3, we increase the segment size for that particular segment by 0.25 seconds at the beginning and end of the audio. We repeat the process until one of the recognizers outputs a confidence score of more than 0.3. We then select the next segment of 0.5 seconds having an overlap of 0.25 seconds with the current optimal segment. The entire process is repeated until the entire audio is segmented. At the end, we combine all the hypotheses generated for each chunk to create an utterance level hypotheses for each ASR.

3.2 Combining ASR hypothesis

We use off-the-shelf monolingual Hindi and Indian English ASRs for decoding speech. To measure the performance of the ASRs on code-switched speech, we test them on an in-house conversational speech corpus consisting of 52k Hindi-English mixed utterances. The corpus is transcribed using the Devanagari script for Hindi words and the Latin script for English words. The English ASR gives a Word Error Rate (WER) of 80% and Hindi ASR gives a WER of 48% on the corpus. The high error rate of both ASRs can be attributed to the difference in script between the reference and hypotheses words as well as the poor performance of monolingual ASRs at code-switch points.

We hypothesize that each ASR will recognize a set of words in the given audio segment, and the collection of the sets will contain all the words present in that particular audio segment. We conduct a quantitative evaluation on 10k code-switched utterances by passing them through both monolingual ASRs and checking whether the ground truth words are present in either of the recognition hypotheses. We obtain a recall of 0.84, which indicates that most words present in the utterance are also present in the output of the two recognizers. We pass each segment obtained through dynamic chunking through Hindi and English monolingual ASRs respectively to obtain two ASR hypotheses for each segment, which we then combine to form utterance level hypotheses.

4 Interface Overview

The annotation interface as shown in figure 2 consists of a button to play audio and a text box. We display the predicted words in a time-linear fashion as clickable blocks. As the user clicks on each word button, all the buttons before and including it becomes disabled, to allow the user to easily focus on the progression of the transcriptions. If the user presses the backspace or attempts to remove certain words, the respective disabled word buttons appear again. Users also have an option of typing out the transcription if they wish to, in both the languages.[1]

If the user wishes to use the keyboard, we also provide quick keyboard shortcuts to improve the efficiency of transcription. These shortcuts allow the user to play/pause the audio, and toggle scripts easily. More details about the interface can be found in the appendix section.

5 Experiments

5.1 Setup

We performed a user study to evaluate the efficacy of our system. We measured transcription quality, annotator effort and the net time taken to transcribe utterances. We compared our annotation

[1]The transliteration is powered by Google's Input Tools API

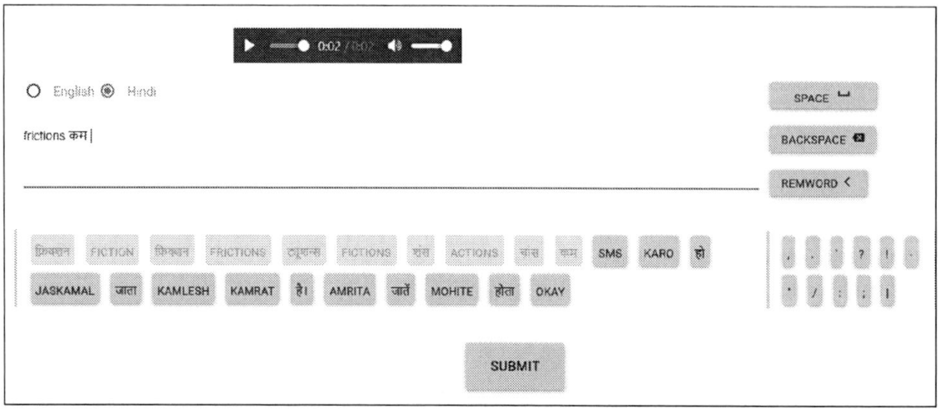

Figure 1: CoSSAT (Code-Switched Speech Annotation Tool)

tool (CoSSAT) against a baseline system, where no ASR hypothesis is shown and the annotators are expected to type out the entire transcription. 10 users annotated 14 code-switched speech utterances. All participants were Hindi-English bilinguals and had no knowledge about the system before conducting the study.

We implemented multiple measures to reduce biases during the annotation task. 4 utterances out of 14 that each user is shown were practice exercises for the annotators to get used to the interface and were not used for the final evaluation. The sequence of the interface (baseline vs. CoSSAT) displayed changed for each user such that each utterance and interface was paired at least five times.

Users were asked to listen to the audio displayed on the page and could play the audio as many times as they wanted. They were asked to transcribe all audible words in the audio sample except speech fillers (e.g., "uh" and "eh"). The users were required to enter the tokens in the script to which they belong - Hindi in Devanagari script and English in Latin script, although this distinction was difficult to make sometimes due to the prevalence of borrowing between the two languages. We did this instead of having all tokens in one script to ensure correctness of transcribed Hindi and English tokens. Often, the transcribing of tokens in a different script can cause certain tokens to be transcribed in different ways (for example), which would have resulted in a cumbersome and misleading evaluation process, even with post-transliteration.

5.2 Quantitative Evaluation

To evaluate our system, we used the following three metrics (1) Transcription Quality (2) Annotation Speed (3) Annotation Effort. For every utterance, we had 10 transcriptions, 5 transcriptions from our proposed interface, and 5 from the baseline interface.

5.2.1 Transcription Quality

Transcription quality was determined by computing word error rate (WER) using a standard procedure[2], using the transcriptions present in our in-house dataset as the gold standard. We calculated WER for the transcriptions created by users using our system as well as for the transcriptions created using the baseline approach. From table 1 we see that transcriptions created using our system have a WER of 19.7%, while the number is much higher for the baseline at 34.74%. After analysing transcripts which had high WER, we noticed that for words where the ASR hypothesis was not present, errors could be attributed to spelling variants, spelling errors, hyphenated words, and grammatical errors. Besides these errors, in the baseline method users made errors in phonetically similar phrases like "of score" instead of "of course".

Another major source of errors was the use of a different script for transcribing a borrowed word, which meant that the annotator used the Hindi script to transcribe a word that was in the Latin script in the reference transcription or vice versa. This is a very challenging problem for transcription of code-switched speech where the two languages are written in different scripts, as it is difficult to make the distinction between loan words and code-switching (Bali et al., 2014).

[2]https://www.nist.gov/itl/iad/mig/rich-transcription-evaluation

To make the comparison fair, we also computed a relaxed WER by converting the transcriptions into phoneme sequences by running a Grapheme to Phoneme (g2p) system on all words and post-processing phoneme sequences. We divided phonemes into classes based on phonetic features and treated each phoneme in a single class as equivalent. If the phoneme classes of all phonemes in a word was the same as those in the reference word, it was treated as a match. This helped take care of minor spelling errors and variants such as long/short vowels and nasalization. Relaxed WER for both systems are reported in table 1. We observe that the relaxed WER numbers for both techniques are significantly lower than the baseline. Crucially, the CoSSAT WER is even lower than the relaxed WER of the baseline, which shows that our interface helps even if we discount the fact that it helps users select the correct spelling variation of a word.

Metrics	CoSSAT	Baseline
WER	19.7%	34.74%
Relaxed WER	9.3%	25.6%

Table 1: WER and relaxed WER for measuring Quality of Transcriptions

5.2.2 Annotation Speed

In the case for transcription task using CoSSAT, we recorded time taken by the user to transcribe from the moment the user clicks on the first word or clicks on the text-box provided to the moment the user clicks submit. In case of the baseline system, we recorded time from the moment the user clicks on the text-box to the moment the user clicks submit. We normalized the time recorded for each audio using the formula (A).

$$\text{Normalized Time } (NT) = \left(\frac{t}{TT}\right) \text{——— (A)}$$

where t is the time taken for transcribing the audio by user X and TT is the total time taken by user X to transcribe all utterances. Figure 2 shows a plot of NT v/s utterance length. We observe that for utterance having ground truth transcriptions of 50 characters or less, CoSSAT takes less time for transcription but for longer utterances, the baseline system is faster. This might be attributed to the fact that longer utterances led to a larger set of word hypothesis resulting in more time for visual search of the tokens across the interface. We intend to address this issue by weeding out improbable suggestions based on confidence and language model scores in future work.

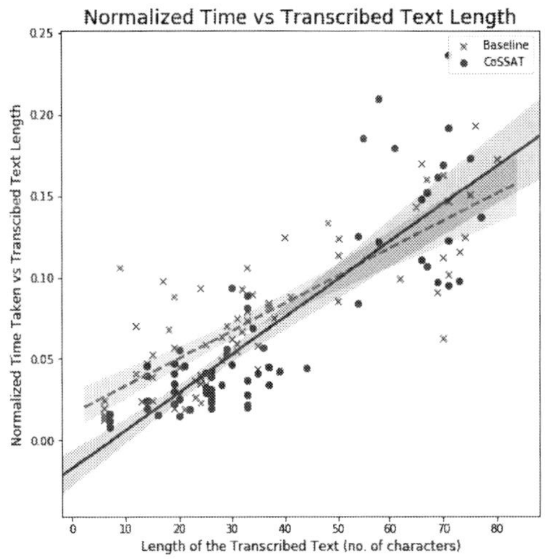

Figure 2: Annotation Speed Plot for each audio. Y axis is the Normalized Time Taken for the utterance. X axis is number of characters present in the utterance. Red colour (cross) is the Baseline system. Blue (dots) colour is CoSSAT.

5.2.3 Annotation Effort

One way to measure annotation effort is to measure the number of keystrokes and mouse clicks. The CoSSAT system resulted in 8 keystrokes and 8 mouse clicks on average, while the baseline system had 57.1 keystrokes and 5.4 mouse clicks. This is explained by the fact that the annotators relied on typing for the baseline interface and clicking on candidate words for the CoSSAT interface, however, overall, the total annotation effort was much lower for the CoSSAT system.

5.3 Qualitative Evaluation

In addition to the metrics collected during the study, users were asked rate their experience on both the interfaces. Questions consisted of rating each system from 1 (worst) to 5(best), on criteria such as Convenience (how easy it was to use), Speed (how fast they felt they could annotate), User-Friendliness (how simple it was to understand the interface), and Error Robustness (how much each system prevented them from making annotation errors). In all cases, the ratings were higher for CoSSAT than the baseline system. Finally, we asked them which system they would prefer using as a potential speech annotator tool. 7 out of 10 annotators said they preferred CoSSAT over the baseline system.

We also asked annotators for feedback and suggestions. One suggestion was to put larger sized or bold buttons for words that had higher probability according to the ASR confidence. Another suggestion was to show candidate words incrementally, rather than all at once. We plan to take this feedback into account while creating the next version of our tool.

6 Conclusion

In this paper, we propose an annotation tool for transcribing code-switched speech, which makes use of dynamic audio chunking and combines ASR hypotheses from two monolingual ASR systems to present candidate words to annotators. We compare our tool to a baseline system where the user has to type the entire transcription using two scripts and find that our proposed system performs better in terms of transcription quality, speed and annotation effort in a user study conducted with 10 annotators. Annotators report that our system is faster, easier to use, more user-friendly and more robust to annotation errors.

In this work, we present the hypotheses from both monolingual ASRs as two-word streams. In future work, we plan to create an aligned structure such as a word lattice and show candidate words to users as they are annotating the utterance instead of all at once. We also plan to collapse cross-transcribed borrowed words in both languages into a single variant using statistics from corpora, so that annotators can be more consistent in annotating such words.

Since our system does not rely on the existence of a code-switched ASR system, it can be used to bootstrap data collection for a code-switched language pair for which monolingual ASRs exist. This can help collect transcribed speech data faster, which can, in turn, help build better code-switched ASR systems.

7 Acknowledgments

We would like to thank all the reviewers' for their valuable comments. We would also like to thank all the users who participated in the user-study.

References

Kalika Bali, Jatin Sharma, Monojit Choudhury, and Yogarshi Vyas. 2014. "i am borrowing ya mixing?" an analysis of english-hindi code mixing in facebook. In *Proceedings of the First Workshop on Computational Approaches to Code Switching*, pages 116–126.

Michael Levit, Yan Huang, Shuangyu Chang, and Yifan Gong. 2017. Don't count on asr to transcribe for you: Breaking bias with two crowds. In *Proc. Interspeech 2017*, pages 3941–3945.

Dau-Cheng Lyu, Tien-Ping Tan, Eng-Siong Chng, and Haizhou Li. 2015. Mandarin–english code-switching speech corpus in south-east asia: Seame. *Language Resources and Evaluation*, 49(3):581–600.

Sanket Shah and Sunayana Sitaram. 2019. Using monolingual speech recognition for spoken term detection in code-switched hindi-english speech. In *ICDM 2019 Workshop on Multilingual Cognitive Services*.

Shan-Ruei You, Shih-Chieh Chien, Chih-Hsing Hsu, Ke-Shiu Chen, Jia-Jang Tu, Jeng Shien Lin, and Sen-Chia Chang. 2004. Chinese-english mixed-lingual keyword spotting. In *2004 International Symposium on Chinese Spoken Language Processing*, pages 237–240.

Sunayana Sitaram, Khyathi Raghavi Chandu, Sai Krishna Rallabandi, and Alan W Black. 2019. A survey of code-switched speech and language processing. *arXiv preprint arXiv:1904.00784*.

Matthias Sperber, Graham Neubig, Satoshi Nakamura, and Alex Waibel. 2016. Optimizing computer-assisted transcription quality with iterative user interfaces. In *Proceedings of the Tenth International Conference on Language Resources and Evaluation (LREC 2016)*, pages 1986–1992, Portorož, Slovenia. European Language Resources Association (ELRA).

Author Index

Aharonov, Ranit, 29
Asahara, Masayuki, 6

Bilu, Yonatan, 29

Colruyt, Camiel, 15

De Clercq, Orphée, 15

Fukumoto, Fumiyo, 24

Hoste, Véronique, 15

Jacovi, Michal, 29
Joshi, Pratik, 48

Kotlerman, Lili, 29

Lavee, Tamar, 29
Li, Jiyi, 24

Orbach, Matan, 29

Park, Jong, 39

Santy, Sebastin, 48
Shah, Sanket, 48
Sitaram, Sunayana, 48
Slonim, Noam, 29

Tratz, Stephen, 1

Yang, Wonsuk, 39
Yoon, Seungwon, 39

Association for Computational Linguistics
209 N. Eighth Street
Stroudsburg, Pennsylvania 18360

ISBN 978-1-7138-0075-0

9 781713 800750

CURRAN ASSOCIATES INC.
proceedings.com